MW01515613

Anthroposophy & Imagination

Selected and Introduced by Kate Farrell
Series Editor: Robert McDermott

CLASSICS FROM THE

Journal for
ANTHROPOSOPHY

NUMBER 76   SUMMER 2006

This volume contains articles from the following issues of the
Journal for Anthroposophy: Zajonc, 1980 (#31); Hughes, 1986 (#43);
Wulsin, 1986 (#43); Bamford, 1981 (#33); Welburn, 1988 (#47 & #48);
Lusseyran, 1968 (#8); Nathan Lyons, 1972 (#15); O'Neil, 1965 (#2);
Tarkovsky, 1985(#42); Kühlewind,1992 (#55); Nick Lyons, 1975 (#22);
Lipson, 1995 (#60); Barfield, 1976 (#24).

We thank Dan Marshall for permission to use his portrait of
Georg Kühlewind. We also thank Trond S. Trondsen from
nostalghia.com for his kind help in obtaining the cover image.

Front cover and layout: Seiko Semones

Series Editor: Robert McDermott

Editor: Kate Farrell

The Journal for Anthroposophy
1923 Geddes Ave., Ann Arbor, MI 48104
TEL 734.662.9355   FAX 734.662.1727

ISSN – 0021-8235

Printed by McNaughton & Gunn, Inc., Saline, Michigan

In Memory of Georg Kühlewind
1924 – 2006

CONTENTS

Introduction

Faithful to Mystery: The Road to Imagination

Kate Farrell

> *This open channel to the highest life is the first and last reality,*
> *so subtle, so quiet, yet so tenacious, that although I have never*
> *expressed the truth, and although I've never heard the expression of it*
> *from any other, I know the whole truth is here for me.*
>
> —Ralph Waldo Emerson

> *Lad of Athens, faithful be*
> *To Thyself,*
> *And Mystery—*
> *All the rest is Perjury—*
>
> —Emily Dickinson

When I was ten or eleven, I made a plan to run away and live in the woods, somehow talking my little sister Margaret into going with me. Despite our fear of the dark, the departure was always set for the middle of the night: the next full moon, say, at 2:30 in the morning. We kept clothes for the trip in a special drawer, but there were few other practical considerations. We knew the general direction of the route: across the road, then up a dirt road; maybe stopping for the night in the big ditch there, then through the woods we knew and beyond.

The idea was no doubt inspired by days spent exploring with our brothers the woods near our house. "All trees say: *Vanish into us*," writes Ptolemy Tompkins in "Those Dark Trees,"[1] and kids know how to accept the invitation; know how to take the hint from an old line of trees and begin the march toward (in Tompkins' words) "the secret heart of the world." The place my sister and I had in mind was that kind of spot: less a place than an atmosphere, the sort that becomes visible mainly in art—a watercolor forest by Paul Klee, maybe, with stairs to mid-air entrances among the trees. On the designated night, we would quietly rise, dress in our special clothes, take a loaf of bread from the pantry and be ready to go. But opening the front door was like waking from a dream: nothing out there but icy darkness. Not tonight, I'd tell Margaret, but soon, I promise, one night very soon.

Our journey, or its mood, shows up often in poetry: *I will arise and go now and go to Innisfree* ... But the trips whose élan most reminds me of our plan are the real-life treks toward paradise recounted by Mircea Eliade. In his book *The Quest*,[2] for instance, Eliade tells the true story of the Guarini Indians' search for The Land without Evil, the world as it was when people walked with the gods. During the 16th century, these South American tribes began looking for their lost homeland, the pure and perfect land of "the beginning," a project that went on for centuries. Certain tribes danced night and day trying to become light enough to fly there, or to obtain knowledge of the route to be taken—the way also taken during prayer and after death, a road at once natural and supernatural.

Had my sister and I thought of it at the time, we would have gladly danced to discover route information or become light enough for the journey. We never, however, actually did set out. Travel conditions remained inauspicious, and, like the Guarinis, we kept rescheduling. I should add that it never felt like a game. On the contrary, the side of myself who dreamed up the plan seemed realer, more serious—and more myself— than the one who inhabited my usual school and church and neighbor- hood existence, with its measured-out possibilities and watchdog-protected darknesses; an existence I was already worried about growing up into.

Then again, misgivings about fitting in seem to have been written into the bones of great numbers of us who grew up in the 50's and 60's, a generation famously determined to trust its own experience, go by its own rules, invent its own lives—have an "original relation to the Universe," in Emerson's wonderful phrase.[3] So that in a way I can picture throngs of us looking out from that childhood door through the dark, wondering how and when and in what direction. At the same time, I can't look back at the plan without thinking I was already headed for poetry.

Once poetry caught me up, it was the creative imagination that suggested itself as the road through the dark toward "the secret heart of the world." But did the road actually lead anywhere? Was imagination just childish fantasy grown up, a backwards journey to illusory paradises, "an amiable insanity," as someone once put it. Or was it, as some thought, the key to that free and original relation we all wanted so badly; not amiable madness but *Mundus Imaginalis*[4] (in Henri Corbin's term); the link, as Owen Barfield thought, between matter and spirit; Emerson's channel to truth, finally open to everyone; light shining in the darkness.

I eventually came to think that imagination was the road I was looking for all along—one that leads through potentially endless levels of understanding, changing the imaginer, and perhaps the world around her, in the direction of an existence there's less reason to run away from. On the other hand, in the case of imagination, direction is destination and however universal the route, the pilgrimage is personal; so that the best and perhaps only way for me to say more about what I mean is to go back to the time when I gave up on the dream forest and discovered poetry.

2.

Was it a vision, or a waking dream?
Fled is that music—Do I wake or sleep?
                    "Ode to a Nightingale," John Keats

Jorge Luis Borges says that he discovered poetry one evening when his father recited "Ode to a Nightingale" in the library of his boyhood home in Buenos Aires. Not a word of the lines did he understand at the time, but he swears he found poetry that night "as a music and a passion." For me, something like that happened during summer visits to Oklahoma, where my roughly educated, gruff-voiced grandfather quoted Whitman and Shakespeare while pointing out the constellations above his dusty little farm. Though I understood Whitman as little as Borges did Keats, I somehow got the idea that poetry was a magical language, one that had once communicated the secrets of existence. From the first, I associated poetry with nature. Like the woods, it had a mystery and freedom that introduced me to my own. And I remember the day it came to me, as I waited for the school bus, that if trees used words instead of limbs and leaves, they'd speak in poetry.

Not until I was a high school senior did I read a modern-sounding poem and realize that real poets were still writing. We students followed along as our English teacher read aloud the poem by E. E. Cummings that begins

> In Just-
> spring when the world is mud-
> luscious …

and ends with the goat-footed balloon man whistling "far/and/wee." After reading the poem, the teacher explained that it was impossible to understand a poem without first analyzing it. In this one, for example, you had to know that the word *goat-footed* symbolized the Greek god Pan. A quiet, shy confrontation-hater, I was surprised to find myself speaking up, saying that I'd understood the poem without analyzing anything. She denied the possibility. What was that *feeling* of understanding, I asked, if not understanding? She had no interest in the question and I, no way of pressing my case. By "understanding," I didn't mean that I'd understood the poem completely, but that the spring fever of its lines had come alive in my mind. Bypassing what was openly conveyed to analyze words on a page seemed as senseless as dissecting springtime without going outside. And I was furious that, for my classmates, poetry was about to become a pointless exercise that had nothing to do with them or their lives. None of this could I say at the time. In any case, the incident, forgettable to all but me, did me the favor of focusing my ordinarily dreamy attention on a question that has stayed with me ever since: what sort of understanding is the understanding of poetry? It got me thinking too about gatehouses of knowledge that prevent instead of enable understanding. Within a few years, I was wondering if my catholic school religion wasn't something like that: a vast gatehouse built at the border of what? The unknowable? Nothingness?

3.

Northrop Frye said that, walking to school one day, he just sloughed off for good the oppressive, man-made picture of god ("that lugubrious old Stinker in the Sky") while holding on to the part of religion that made deep sense to him.[5] A lightning flash like that could have saved me endless trouble. The best I could do was to nervously ask myself the obvious questions. Wouldn't all-wise spiritual beings give us a way to know about them directly, instead of requiring faith in not-necessarily-trustworthy authorities? Was there no better way to become a better person than by avoiding church-defined sins? One Sunday in college, I borrowed a car to attend a go-through-the-motions church service—and kept driving: out to the autumn woods which seemed so much holier. Then after quitting school to get married and "live my own life" (as we thought of it back then) I felt obliged to face, at least as a possibility, the terrifying pitch blackness of a world without meaning and a life without purpose. Before long, I had (unlike Frye) thrown the baby out with the holy water, so to speak, and like so many others who did the same thing, I had no idea that once religion was out of the picture, the ego, in a stupendous variety of disguises, would be ready to run the show; no thought that relying on my own thinking required making my thinking reliable; or that things like goodness, truth, freedom and love were tricky achievements, as distant and elusive as that magic land in the forest.

Skip ahead a few years, and I'm a mixed-up, grief-stricken, old-feeling 27-year-old widow, living with my two little kids in New York City where I'd come to study literature at Columbia. By then, I was writing poetry seriously, and questions about how and whether and how much we can know had a practical urgency. My husband had committed suicide the year before (his manic depression, clear in retrospect, never diagnosed) and, within a few months of my arrival in Manhattan, my closest childhood friend would die in a motorcycle accident. I was counting on poetry—along with whatever secrets waited behind the doors of the big city—to help me tell my children why life was worth living.

As it turned out, those first years in New York were not unlike the years Kathleen Raine reported spending at Cambridge back in the 20's. After growing up surrounded by "the poetry of life" in a family where imaginative vision was second nature, she had capitulated to the positivism that dominated Cambridge in its so-called golden age. It took half her life, she said, to rid herself of what she learned there and make her way back to Yeats and Blake and "those states of consciousness through which alone the lost paradise of the imagination can be regained."[6]

At Columbia, I was as annoyed as ever that so little attention was paid to what writers had to say before their work was torn into. But my inarticulate inklings about a more imaginative approach was no match for the materialism that, as Raine said, was the real religious faith of the 20th century. The overall message gained here and there in and out of class was something like this: no sophisticated, intellectually honest, post-Freudian thinker would waste her time reading or writing to find or express any sort of lasting truth. Yes, literature and the arts, along with love and beauty, were the very things that made life worth living, providing a temporary respite (no doubt evolutionary in origin) from life's disappointments and miseries. But once we knew that our minds belonged to our bodily machinery, we knew that poetic vision, like the madness of religion, had nowhere to come from but the boxed-in subjectivity of a fantasy-prone brain. Readers and writers of the past had the excuse of ignorance, but those of today had none. Who was I to disagree? By the time I graduated, I could almost think of myself as a thinker who knew enough not to hope for the truth. Almost. For I led a double life—memorizing lines with the opposite message, turning to books by poets like Rilke and Yeats during emergencies of everyday meaninglessness, and never completely giving up on poetry's hints of who-knows-what saving reality; dim lights shining back through dark trees.

4.

There's a kind of dream in which you discover new rooms in your old house, rooms that are not only beautiful and interesting, but also strangely familiar. For me, the rooms in those dreams seem to stand for openings-up to new understandings—the moving past a wall that isn't a wall after all—that comes through imaginative experience. "The imagined world," writes Gaston Bachelard, "gives us an expanding home..." When I began to teach, especially a college workshop called "Imaginative Reading and Writing," I found that once students began to have this kind of experience, it was smooth sailing.

By now, I felt sure that imaginative reading was a creative activity that was as different from ordinary reading as imaginative writing was from newspaper prose, that imaginative works made this kind of reading possible as naturally as aquatic buoyancy made floating above the ground possible. All it took on the part of the reader was sympathetic receptivity—whereas a closed, critical attitude was like wearing iron shoes into the water. This way of reading would be second nature, I thought, if literature weren't used so exclusively for teaching critical (as opposed to imaginative) thinking and writing. As it was, it took my pressured Columbia students half a semester to remove their iron shoes and wade in and see that the inspired state of mind belonged, not just to writing, but to reading and the contemplation that went with it, that these activities were all of a piece; inspiring, sustaining and shedding light on each other. They saw too that imagination strengthened with use, helping them think more clearly and deeply, not only about books but about everything else in life.

When asked around this time to write a poetry textbook, I decided to first figure out all I could about the workings of imagination, which by then seemed to be at the heart of what poetry was actually *for*. Complicating matters was the fact that I was still living a double life— "willingly suspending disbelief" while reading, yet holding on to an obligatory disbelief as my official point of view. It was a collision course. All this time, for example, I'd been secretly hoping that science would eventually find (and prove true) the hidden side of life. But what if scientific thinking could only find the outsides of things—while the perhaps no-less-real things poetry disclosed *required* imaginative investigation and expression? A possibility that suggested, what else? *spiritual* realities and purposes. *Spiritual*: I despised the very word. And with supernatural beings out of the question, what or whose purposes were they? I was becoming somewhat paranoid. Was I trying to know something that wasn't meant to be known?

Then one day my husband Bob picked up a copy of Owen Barfield's *History in English Words* from the front counter of Books & Company, one of Manhattan's legendary now-vanished literary bookstores. Later that day, I was taking in sentences I'd been waiting all my life for, and over the next couple of years I slowly worked my way through the store's complete set of Barfield paperbacks. Having always assumed that philosophy was too abstract for me, I found that Barfield's work had the effect of poetry. There was the familiar "felt change of consciousness" (Barfield's term for the shift to another state of mind). And, as with poetry, just following the words brought a gradual understanding of things that had at first seemed beyond me—"Suddenly I had the right eyes," says Rilke about catching on to Cezanne's painting. The only drawback being that Barfield's stranger ideas seemed a risk to my sanity.

Having put off Barfield's novel *Unancestral Voice*[7] till last, one September Sunday, I read it straight through, absolutely riveted, not bothering to stop for what I didn't understand (which was plenty), completely caught up in the mystery of the Meggid. The Meggid is an invisible mental visitor who, early in the book, strikes up an inner conversation with Burgeon (the Barfield-like protagonist), offering cryptic hints about the secrets of existence, leaving Burgeon to work out the details for himself. A phrase like "interior is anterior" (that is, mind precedes matter) sets Burgeon to digging around in literature and history and gathering hints from everyday events and chance conversations while feeling his way through a series of incremental epiphanies.

Along the way, the reader learns about, among other things, the evolution of consciousness, Barfield's big subject. To sum up an idea that resists summation: ancient cultures felt themselves to be participants in a spirit-and-meaning-permeated universe. That sort of inspired group consciousness gradually narrowed to our current self-enclosed consciousness, in which, in Matthew Arnold's words, "we mortal millions live alone," yanked by our thinking toward a dispiriting literalism, egotism and materialism. On the positive side, this inner evolution made possible, not only the successes of modern science, but the potential for true freedom, creative love and further stages of knowledge—including a stage where "the lost paradise of the imagination" might be regained, this time freely and consciously.

As *Unancestral Voice* progresses, the Meggid tells Burgeon that the Word, the Logos, has been the secret "transforming agent" in the evolutionary processes of both nature and consciousness. The incarnation of the Logos, he says, was the turning point of time, after which the responsibility for evolution was gradually being entrusted to human beings. Imperiling this vast and risky process was "the great taboo" against knowing spiritual realities on our own. Our usual self-understanding, according to the Meggid, is a sort of lifeless cover story, a shallow mirror behind which we're afraid to look, instinctively dreading to face our own destructiveness. But daring to face the worst in ourselves, we would find something else—the source of our own thinking, the inner word or logos, the creative spirit through which we could change ourselves and the world now entrusted to us.

On that September Sunday, I'd caught on to the barest gist of something like that in a disorderly, excited, walking-around-the-ceiling kind of way, when it dawned on me that I'd been *living* the great taboo. That my default agnosticism (to which my fear of "going crazy" from reading Barfield belonged) was my own cover story, that deep down I knew for a fact that his trustworthy voice would more likely drive a reader to sanity than to madness. My real fear was that taking his ideas to heart would make people *think* that I was going mad (or else "taking the easy way out"), both the believers from my religious past and the disbelievers from my agnostic present. All my relationships seemed to be at stake, and what would become of my writing? There I was, in my own darkness behind my own shallow mirror. "The soul," writes Yeats, "must become its own betrayer, its own deliverer, the mirror turn lamp…"

In the book's final paragraphs, the Meggid at last identifies himself,[8] describing his part in an intricate reverse hierarchy of mutual service: beings who serve the Logos who, in turn, serves everyone else with a washing-of-the-feet selflessness. The three final words, set off by themselves on the page

I am

yours

were like a message passed through those ranks to the Meggid to Barfield to me—and who was I but the Prodigal in the pigsty.

One last hesitation: what if Barfield were mistaken. What if I made some grand effort only to be sucked back with everyone and everything else into lifeless nothingness. But by then I knew that reading Barfield "as if" spiritual truth were knowable would make me a better, saner, more useful person. That alone made me less afraid of death, even a death into nothingness. And finally it was just a matter of giving up my double life, my pretense that the search for truth wasn't built into every serious thought I'd ever had and every serious word I'd ever read or spoken.

5.

"Between two worlds life hovers like a star," writes Byron, in a line that sums up what countless poems, myths, teachings and traditions, in one way or another, assume or hint or say. That we belong to two worlds: the invisible, hard-to-know eternal one we come from and the noisy, obvious, temporal one all around us. According to Plato's myth, we forget the first one when we drink from Lethe, the river of forgetfulness, before whizzing off like shooting stars to be born. But "not in entire forgetfulness" do we come, as Wordsworth put it, and people through the ages have tried in all kinds of ways to remember or know or find that other world while still in this one. Once shamans climbed magic ropes and special trees to get there, and whole tribes, like the homesick Guarinis, spent their lives looking for a road in that direction. As consciousness evolved, the distance between the worlds kept growing, so that today it's easy to feel, with Matthew Arnold, that we are homeless travelers

> Wandering between two worlds; one dead,
> The other powerless to be born

… a rift that in Rilke's poem "Evening" has sunk deep inside us:

> The evening slowly changes into the clothes
> held for it by a row of ancient trees;
> and you watch as one world rises toward heaven
> and the other sinks down beneath your feet
>
> leaving you not at home in either one;
> not quite so dark as those silent houses
> but not testifying to eternity with the passion
> of that part that turns to a star at night and rises
>
> leaving you (speechlessly to disentangle)
> your life, vast and frightened and changing,
> so that now closed-in, now all-encompassing
> your life is sometimes a stone in you, sometimes a star.

In Barfield's view, imagination can reconnect the two worlds, the stone and the star. For imagination is the bridge between matter and spirit. On first hearing this idea, I pictured the link as one of those worn footbridges between mountain peaks in old Chinese paintings. But Barfield depicts it, not as a solid bridge, but as a rainbow of imaginative activity "spanning the two precipices and linking them harmoniously together."[9] The chasm the rainbow spans is modern everyday consciousness. Caught in that gap, we believe only what our senses tell us: that matter is nothing but physical matter, while spirit either doesn't exist or defies understanding. Whereas from the rainbow bridge of imaginative activity we can become aware that matter, including our own bodies, is *coagulum spiritus*—that part of the spirit that physical senses can perceive—while spirit is (among other things) the one who is doing the perceiving. For Barfield and Rudolf Steiner, as for Blake, Coleridge, Henri Corbin, Kathleen Raine and others, true imagination, unlike mere fantasy, is an experience or capacity or way of thinking that "unveils," as Corbin put it, "the hidden reality." Luckily, certain writings help unveil it for the rest of us, drawing us toward the more-than-rational state in which they were written—and toward "sympathetic participation" (Barfield's term) in the thinking that created them. To this almost indescribable inner conversation—different every time for every reader—you bring not just your intellect but your whole mind and life. As a rule, there are lots of long pauses and mental digressions, as you connect what is said to your own experience, put things into your own words, picture them in your own way, and otherwise "dwell in possibility," in Dickinson's phrase. One passage seems to say something you've always wanted to say; another opens up a new part of the world—and a new part of yourself along with it. Sometimes there's just the barest premonition of understanding; other times, the meaning, obvious enough while you're reading, vanishes the minute you turn the page. Coming back to the page several books later, the meaning is clear as day. Ideas come from nowhere, answering unrelated questions, filling in the larger picture. As understandings from one book sink into, enlarge, alter, and reverberate through those from various others, it's like a taste of that library in heaven (to adapt Donne's image) where all the books open to one another. As for which writing allows this kind of reading, you know it by its effect. For me, it cuts across genres, from poetry to certain works of fiction, imaginative philosophy, creative scholarship, and other kinds of prose.

In *Surprised by Joy*, C. S. Lewis recalls a day when he referred to philosophy as "a subject" in front of his friends Bede Griffiths and Owen Barfield. "It wasn't a *subject* to Plato," Barfield remarked; "it was a way." Nowadays someone could go to school for a very long time without discovering that poetry, say, or philosophy is "a way"—meaning of course a way to the truth. But it's that kind of quest that gives this kind of reading its momentum, passion, joy, and efficacy. It's a quest in which, as van Gogh says about the artistic quest, you never stop looking for something you never completely find. Every stage is interesting and important, not because more and more facts are at your disposal (which may happen as well), but because you are gradually answering your own deepest questions, finding out what you yourself think, discovering new square footage in the expanding home of consciousness, brightening the light that is, in Emerson's words, "supplied by the observer."

In a way, it's like drinking little by little from the River of Unforgetting. The Greek word *a-létheia*—literally un-forgetting—was the word for truth when Plato pursued it; the truth that Christ told Pilate he had come to bear witness to. Georg Kühlewind emphasizes that in those days *alétheia* didn't mean truth as "correctness" but was at once a spiritual reality and the thinking that unveiled it; it was imaginative thinking, living thinking; thinking that moves through progressively deeper states and stages of consciousness; it was recognition as well as discovery.[10] The idea of truth as an expedition into mystery is there too in my title poem:

> Lad of Athens, faithful be
> To Thyself,
> And Mystery—
> All the rest is Perjury—

Dickinson's lines address, I think, the Lad of Athens in us all—the one who, in the days of the Greek Mysteries, would have gladly vowed silence for the sake of enlightenment. The poem urges, however, not silence, but a double promise: to be true to ourselves (our own firsthand experience) and to mystery—the knowable unknown, the door through which the unconscious becomes conscious. In keeping both oaths at once, we would be evolving witnesses to an unfolding truth, our deepening capacities deepening the mystery (and the self) toward and into and through which we move. "All the rest"—presumably every thought, word and action—is perjury. Clinging to fixed truths would be perjury. And convincing others to do so: well, that would be suborning perjury! No death penalty for the divulger of knowledge, but the journey of unforgetting remains an endless odyssey.

<h2 style="text-align:center">6.</h2>

Imagine that, instead of a starfish regenerating its missing appendage (a common occurrence), the appendage were to rebuild, not only its missing starfish body, but its whole lost undersea kingdom. Something like that happens in Rilke's poem "Archaic Torso of Apollo": a fragment of an ancient statue of the god of truth and light begins to glow like a lantern, then shine like a star, finally disclosing a living universe that gazes back at the gazer. When this poem shows up in the last chapters of Ptolemy Tompkins' memoir *Paradise Fever*,[11] it begets a similar epiphany —and a contemporary account of the transformative power of imaginative reading.

For much of the book, Tompkins the child has been swept along by the funny-in-retrospect adventures of his famous New Age father, whose symptoms of "paradise fever" include captaining a naked boat crew in search of the lost continent of Atlantis—and insisting on having two wives. But the core of the book is the author's childhood discovery of a secret "world-behind-the-world," a realm about which he constantly dreams and guesses, linking it with long ago ages and the mysteries of nature; a near-yet-far dimension for which he feels—despite huge fears of its unknown intentions—a deep affinity and homesickness. Much less at home in the material dimension, by the final scenes he's a worn-out, miserable 33-year-old writer who relies on drugs and alcohol to endure normal existence. Home for a visit, he heads into the woods one hot summer morning, veins full of chemistry, with a warm six pack of beer, a copy of Rudolf Steiner's *Cosmic Memory*[12] (for a writing project about Atlantis) and a book of Rilke's poetry. After swigging a few beers, he opens Rilke at random to "Evening"—the poem quoted earlier about the abyss between worlds—then to the Apollo poem, focusing on the lines that have stopped so many readers in their tracks:

> ... there isn't anyplace that isn't
> Looking at you. You must change your life.

For Tompkins, the words awaken a familiar sensation—"at the exact midpoint between joy and fear," the feeling of being watched by the hidden side of life—but also awaken a way of thinking that, over the course of the day, bridges the rift between worlds, visible and invisible, and makes new sense of life. He thinks about Atlantis and its post-paradise inhabitants, trying to manage by themselves when the gods are out of sight. Maybe, he thinks, if we could keep in mind, even in our very worst hours, the secret world-behind-the-world always out there watching, we could "live down here without its hurting so much." The next day, he drives away from the flawed paradise of childhood and the fake heavens of addiction, to change (the book predicts) in ways he had-n't thought possible.

Nostalgia for paradise, suggests Barfield, is nostalgia for non-physical existence, of which paradise is the symbol, for the "matterless universe from which we all spring." [13] Finishing *Paradise Fever*, I had the feeling that the rift-healing dimension found by Rilke and Tompkins—call it *mundus imaginalis*, the dimension linking earth to the matterless universe—was the land the naked Atlantis-hunters were, without knowing it, seeking, as were my sister and I, and even perhaps the endlessly-dancing Guarinis.

One more story about reading. Once, immersed in a book by Nicholas Berdyaev, I stopped to read my husband a particularly remarkable passage —whereupon it instantly lost its magic, becoming a dull string of empty words. As I sat there perplexed, a funny thing happened: the lines of words on the page began to resemble those rickety roll-fences that keep beach dunes from blowing away. Not sand, in this case, was held in place but expanses of meaning stretching back into the page, a place (or really, state) where a nomad like me could pitch her tent and think—the sort of delicately-anchored mind-to-mind state that a reader, like a lover, half-creates, half-discovers. And for a minute or two, I could feel the difference it made: to be in that state or stranded outside it in everyday thinking; to take part, or not, in the miraculous interchange. Berdyaev said that there are two ways out of our modern aloneness: one is love; the other, communion in the mysteries of existence. The kind of reading I'm talking about seems to be both at once.

7.

In 1817, John Keats wrote in a letter to a friend: "I am certain of nothing but of the holiness of the Heart's affections and the truth of Imagination." But in what *way* is imagination true? The Romantic Movement fell apart, according to Barfield, because its poets and philosophers couldn't adequately answer that question—even those like Shelley and Coleridge for whom imagination was "a passion, a religion, a veritable key to the promised land." The answer had to wait, he says, for Rudolf Steiner to take up where Coleridge left off, proving by his life-work that imagination, when taken seriously, "is the most precious of our possessions," that it "does not merely sustain and please us," but makes us better able to serve our fellow human beings and our age. [14] For Steiner understood that imagination is "a part, and but the first part, of a long sober process of cognition," a process that, in overcoming the divide between subject and object, matter and spirit, can also help us overcome the horrible predicaments that our alienated, materialistic mentality keeps getting us into. [15]

When I first read Steiner, I was surprised to find that, despite a style that seemed miles away from the "poetic," his writing, like Barfield's, had the effect of poetry. Some years later, I discovered that Barfield, when first reading Steiner, had the same experience. [16] It was a while before I realized the obvious: that works written directly out of "more-than-rational" experience, whatever their style or genre, tend to inspire a more-than-rational response—unless something gets in the way. Some works take us only a little beyond everyday thinking, while others can lead much further. Conversely, trying to take in more-than-rational works with "merely rational" thinking can turn gold to straw, making writing that would otherwise be alive, illuminating and transformative seem difficult, inertly informational or even nonsensical.

Steiner deliberately expressed his ideas in a way that would lead to the state of mind in which they could best be understood. He wrote

Philosophy of Freedom, for instance, with the hope of helping to bring about the free spiritual activity it depicts. [17] Still, readers seem to have trouble leaving behind the kind of thinking that Steiner hoped to free them from. Perhaps partly because our literal times and educations strap on the iron shoes of abstraction so firmly and early; partly because Steiner's extraordinary assertions are so transfixing that it's tempting to stop short and simply believe them—or else reject them out of hand—and partly because what he is doing is so new.

Barfield contends that it is "a kind of betrayal" of Steiner to believe him. He "poured out his assertions," says Barfield, "because he trusted his hearers *not* to believe." To become an anthroposophist, he continues, is to use the words of Steiner (as well as those of other writers), to raise ourselves "to a kind of thinking which is itself beyond words, which *precedes* them, in the sense that ideas, words, sentences, propositions are subsequently *drawn out of it*"; it is "to refrain from uniting oneself with words in the humble hope of uniting oneself with the Word."[18]

This special issue of the *Journal for Anthroposophy* brings together a group of thinkers who have moved well past the factual facade of Steiner's work and into its rich interior. They range from the physicist Arthur Zajonc, who explores the synthesis of poetry and science in Goethe's work, to the world-renowned "poet of cinema" Andrei Tarkovsky, who ponders the influence of Steiner on his film *The Sacrifice*. Three other great imaginers—Emerson, Novalis and W.B. Yeats—are the subjects of essays by Gertrude Reif Hughes, Christopher Bamford, and Andrew Welburn, respectively. Among the several books reviewed is R. J. Reilly's marvelous *Romantic Religion*, recently republished by Lindisfarne Press. In "Anthroposophy and Psychoanalysis" writer/psychologist Michael Lipson makes a clear-eyed comparison of the two, while in "Love and Fear," Georg Kühlewind—to whom this collection is dedicated—writes about how "living thinking" can bring the New Testament back to life for today's readers. Concluding the volume is Barfield's remarkable account of how evidence unearthed during his study of language led to his abandoning agnosticism.

Barfield once closed an essay by saying that the end of the path "from the spiritual in the human being to the spiritual in the universe" cannot be reached by one person here and there but only by us all "in fellowship and communion." [19]

> Every person is a half-open door
> Leading to a room for everyone

writes Tomas Tranströmer in "The Half-finished Heaven." [20] It is my experience that "sympathetic participation" in works of imagination by a wide variety of writers (Steiner as well as others) makes all of them clearer—as if the way to that vast democracy of light Steiner envisioned passes naturally through such roomfuls of mutually opening doors.

8.

When the second tower fell on 9/11, I saw it happen from my Brooklyn apartment window and, at the same time, on the television screen right beside it. Even that seemed symbolic. Minutes later, flaming to-do lists drifted across the river into our building's back yard. Even those of us who lost no one we knew took it personally. It was like getting word of a beloved relative's fatal illness—except that, in this case, it was our whole world whose days appeared to be numbered. In the weeks that followed, the beautiful September light around the smoldering skyline seemed to belong to a lost kingdom—or a vast chance squandered. The newspapers, with their shallow talk of war and revenge, just deepened the feeling. How much time did we have? Then came the news that New Yorkers were turning to poetry. What is the mysterious solace of poetry? *The New York Times* asked. But was it solace we were after?

I think of Jacques Lusseyran, the blind French resistance leader and concentration camp survivor who said that, in Buchenwald, poetry made the difference between who survived and who didn't. There, poetry was not literature but medicine; "it tied earth back to heaven," lending prisoners its wings, its inner freedom. The soul dies first, he said, and poetry kept their souls alive against all odds. [21] "It is difficult/ to get the news from poems," wrote William Carlos Williams, "yet men die miserably every day / for lack / of what is found there."

For Barfield, what is found in poetry and other works of imagination is the thinking whose development is the hope of humanity, the power whereby the world "powerless to be born" might be born after all. We cannot change the world, he says, by "tinkering with the outside"; it can only be changed from within, and we *are* its within.[22] Altered eyes, as Blake says, alter everything. In those first post-disaster months, I couldn't help thinking that poetry-reading New Yorkers were searching instinctively for something like that: new eyes, deeper answers; a way of thinking adequate to the situation. And I felt lucky that I could turn, not only to poetry, but to the prose of writers like those I've mentioned here.

In closing, a word about my sister Margaret, childhood traveling companion, now a clinical psychologist who works with the poor and mentally ill in Northern California, many of them near the ends of their ropes. To be of real help, she says, she needs what she gets from metaphysics and meditation. We trade books. And for both of us, opening certain volumes has something of the mystery of opening the door into the dark on those long ago nights—only, these nights travel conditions are propitious and, sooner or later, the road between stone and star starts to come into sight.

Notes

1. Ptolemy Tompkins, "Those Dark Trees," *The Sun, September* 2004; reprinted in *Best Spiritual Writing 2005*, edited by Philip Zaleski.

2. Mircea Eliade, *The Quest: History and Meaning in Religion* (Chicago: University of Chicago Press. 1969), 101-111.

3. "The forgoing generations beheld God and nature face to face; we, through their eyes. Why should not we also enjoy an original relation to the universe? Why should not we have a poetry and philosophy of insight and not of tradition, and a religion by revelation to us, and not the history of theirs." From *Nature*.

4. The Imaginal World

5. David Cayley, *Northrop Frye in Conversation* (Toronto: House of Anansi, 1992), 3-4. Frye, a great literary critic, was also an ordained minister.

6. Kathleen Raine, "Yeats' Singing School," *Yeats the Initiate* (London: Georg Allen & Unwin Ltd., 1986), 439.

7. Owen Barfield, *Unancestral Voice* (Middletown, CT: Wesleyan University Press, 1965). A review of the book appears on p. 85 of this volume.

8. *In Romantic Religion* (recently reprinted by Lindisfarne Press) R. J. Reilly suggests that the Meggid is the "philosophic imagination." See review on p. 82 of this volume.

9. Owen Barfeld, "Matter, Imagination, and Spirit," *The Rediscovery of Meaning and Other Essays* (Middletown, CT: Wesleyan University Press, 1977), 150.

10. See "Love and Fear" on p. 94 of this volume and Ch.10 of *Becoming Aware of the Logos* (Great Barrington, MA: Lindisfarne Press, 1985).

11. Ptolemy Tompkins, *Paradise Fever* (New York: Avon Books, 1997).

12. Two pages earlier (*Paradise Fever*, 269), Tompkins has written: "… Steiner was to my mind far and away the most fascinating intellect among the occultists. … The way I saw it, Rudolf Steiner was where it all either came together or fell apart as far as things New Age were concerned."

13. Said through the character Burgeon in *Worlds Apart* (Middletown, CT: Wesleyan University Press, 1963), 123-124.

14. Owen Barfield, "From East to West," *Romanticism Comes of Age*, (Middletown, CT: Wesleyan University Press, 1966), 45-46.

15. *Romanticism*, 15-16.

16. See, for instance, *Romanticism*, 13 and "Owen Barfield and the History of Language" *Towards* 1, no. 3 (December 1978): 13.

17. See particularly Otto Palmer, *Rudolf Steiner on His Book The Philosophy of Freedom* (Spring Valley, NY: Anthroposophic Press, 1975).

18. "Speech, Reason and Imagination," *Romanticism Comes of Age*, 77.

19. "Man, Thought and Nature," *Romanticism*, 240. Steiner's description of anthroposophy as "a path of knowledge from the spiritual in the human being to the spiritual in the universe" is quoted earlier in that essay.

20. Tomas Tranströmer, *The Half-finished Heaven*, Chosen and Translated by Robert Bly (Saint Paul: Graywolf Press).

21. "Poetry and Buchenwald," *Against the Pollution of the I* (New York: Parabola Books, 1999), 172-175. An excerpt from Lusseyran's autobiography *And There Was Light* appears on p. 78 of this volume. Williams' lines are from "Asphodel, that Greeny Flower."

22. Owen Barfield, *History, Guilt, and Habit,* (Middletown, CT: Wesleyan University Press), 92.

Science and Poetry: Goethe's Synthesis

Arthur G. Zajonc

Goethe presented his ideas on science over one hundred and fifty years ago. His thought has remained an historical-scientific curiosity. Frequently lumped together with the scientific work of such other German poets and philosophers as Herder, Novalis and Schelling, it is termed *Naturphilosophie* and often declared to be a reaction to the rationalism of the Enlightenment. Certainly few scientists have chosen Goethe's viewpoint as their own, although more recently an indication of sympathy can be discerned in the philosophical essays of physicists Werner Heisenberg[1] and Walter Heitler[2] among others.

In sharp contrast with the evaluations of history, Goethe placed more value on his scientific work than his poetic. In this vein we can repeat the oft quoted remark Goethe made to his secretary Eckermann on February 19, 1829, three years before his death:

> I do not pride myself at all on the things I have done as a poet. There have been excellent poets during my lifetime; still more excellent ones lived before me, and after me there will be others. But I am proud that I am the only one in my century who knows the truth about the difficult science of color, and in this I am conscious of being superior to many.

In his introduction to *Goethe's Natural Scientific Writings*, which he edited in the 1890s, Rudolf Steiner concurs with Goethe's evaluation and states that "the natural science of the future lies in the development of Goethe's basic conceptions."[3] If we are to resolve this conflict of opinion we must evaluate the place and significance of Goethean science in the development of science as a whole. The purpose of this paper will be to sketch, at least in its outlines, the pivotal position which Goethean science holds as a necessary cultural-scientific inquiry. The special significance of

Goethean science for anthroposophical thought will only be indicated here, but will find a fuller treatment in a future article. From our considerations I hope it will become evident that Goethe's science was not a reaction *against* genuine scientific inquiry but rather a development of its own methods which will ultimately enable us to reach consciously beyond purely physical investigations to objective research into the moral and spiritual laws that guide human growth and destiny, and which reach into all of Nature's kingdoms and world evolution. Without this understanding of ourselves and our world, we stand as children totally dependent on the grace of God, unable to help Him help us. With this understanding, we can become the conscious cause of our own evolution; with it, we can strive to make of our Earth the star which it longs to become.

In the centuries since the birth of Western civilization in ancient Greece, human thought has gradually shifted from a god-filled cosmology to a view of Nature shorn of the spirit. Newton's law of universal gravitation demonstrated that the same law governed the fall of an apple and the orbit of the moon. The many stunning successes of seventeenth- and eighteenth-century science led to the conviction that indeed all of Nature would one day be explained as a vast mechanism based on the principles of attraction and repulsion (gravitational or electrical). To external sight, the world that surrounded Socrates in the sixth century B.C. and the one that confronted Laplace in the seventeenth were essentially the same; but as human beings continued to gaze into that world, it was as though their eyesight had changed or withered. The night sky with its stars and planets was no longer the dwelling place of gods and the stage of myth. Nor was it fitted with crystal spheres comprised of quintessential substance. Rather the sky, the Earth and we ourselves slowly came to be seen as born out of a primeval material nebula and governed by purely mechanistic laws.

The logical culmination of scientific materialism and its mechanistic worldview was attained during the last half of the eighteenth century in the so-called Enlightenment: a period self-proclaimed by its leading authors as "The Age of Reason," in contrast with the darkness and barbarism that had been humanity's previous plight. During this period, the great discoveries and theories set forth by such figures as Kepler, Galileo, Newton and Benjamin Franklin made their way abroad. This was done not by the efforts of the scientists themselves but rather by those who popularized and published: men of letters such as Voltaire, and the French *philosophes* such as Diedrot and Fontenelle. Roving scientist-magicians brought the marvelous phenomena of the new science to the intelligentsia of Europe and America. Every salon in Paris was filled with conversation about the new cosmology and psychology. Even in far-off Frankfurt, the young Goethe attempted (unsuccessfully) the construction of a then novel electrical apparatus. The worldview which is now a commonplace was then a novelty which caused great excitement. The world was seen as pure mechanism operating on Newtonian (or in Paris, Cartesian) principles. Fontenelle could say: "I esteem the universe all the more since I have known that it is like a watch. It is surprising that Nature, admirable as it is, is based on such simple things." Nor must we imagine that plants, animals and humans beings were exempt from Fontenelle's timepiece; for although Descartes placed the human spirit beyond the extended material world (*res extensa*), Hobbes, Locke and their successors did not. La Mettrie was to write: "The human body is a clock, but an immense one and constructed with so much artifice and skill that if the wheel which turns the second hand should stop, the minute hand would still turn on and continue on its way. ..."

One can justly wonder whether the reaction of the poet followed that of the philosophers. Perhaps unexpectedly we find that poets, too, initially embraced the "New Philosophy." Alexander Pope wrote in his "Epitaph Intended for Sir Isaac Newton":

> Nature and Nature's laws lay hid in night;
> God said, "Let Newton be!" and all was light.

During the first half of the eighteenth century the poets were essentially unanimous in their welcome of the New Philosophy which freed them from the illusory nature of the sense world and gave them truth. The discoveries of Newton were deemed so great that John Hughes could write in 1717:

> The great Columbus of the skys I know!
> 'Tis Newton's soul, that daily travels here
> In search of knowledge for Mankind below.
> O Stay, thou happy Spirit, stay
> And lead me on thro' all the unbeaten Wilds of Day.

Newton's vision was seen as penetrating to the very core of existence and thus providing the poet with the beacon of truth which before had been found in myth and in Nature as it appeared to the senses.

Yet even as the Enlightenment gained momentum in the second half of the century, such sentiments began to change. In 1817, Benjamin Haydon in Britain wrote in his diary:

> The immortal dinner came off in my painting room. Wordsworth was in fine cue, and we had a glorious set-to on Homer, Shakespeare, Milton and Virgil. Lamb got exceedingly merry and exquisitely witty, and his fun in the midst of Wordsworth's solemn intonations of oratory was like the sarcasm and wit of the fool in the intervals of Lear's passions.

> ... He then in a strain of humor beyond description, abused me for putting Newton's head into my picture; "a fellow," said he, "who believed nothing unless it was as clear as the three sides of a triangle." And then he and Keats agreed that he had destroyed all the poetry of the rainbow by reducing it to its prismatic colors. It was impossible to resist him and we all drank "Newton's health, a confusion to mathematics."

Keats later expressed these same sentiments in his oft quoted lines from *Lamia* (229-237):

> Do not all charms fly
> At the mere touch of cold philosophy?
> Philosophy will clip an Angel's wings
> Conquer all mysteries by rule and line,
> Empty the haunted air, the gnomed mine –
> Unweave a rainbow

Across the channel in Jena, August Wilhelm Schlegel played host to similar gatherings. Besides his brother Friedrich, his visitors included the young poet Novalis, the theologian Schliermacher, the poet Tieck, the scientist Steffens and on rare occasions even the great master himself, Goethe. Here they spoke of the inevitable victory of the new poetry of the heart over eighteenth-century rationalism. Clearly these are not the sentiments with which Newton's theories were initially welcomed. By the time Euler, Lagrange and Laplace had finished their elaboration of Newtonian mechanics in France, the deterministic vision they represented was already being rejected by Romantic poets in England and Germany. But if poets could no longer look towards the scientist for inspiration, to whom could they turn? The answer was to Nature itself and to that which it called forth in the human being.

In place of the "truth" given by science, the poet turned to the pure, pristine sensory reality of nature unencumbered by hypothesis and mechanism. The culture of the folk began to replace that of the intelligentsia, for here was to be found the simple immediate joys and truths untainted by the trappings of mechanistic philosophy. Thus Herder encouraged Goethe to search out the popular folklore and poetic tradition of the Alsace region around Strasbourg to find that poetry was not for the cultivated alone, but "poetry in general was a gift to the world and nations." Truth was still being sought but now by an intuitive path quite different from the path of the "discursive intellect." Novalis recognized this contrast and expressed it in a fragment:

> The raw discursive thinker is a scholastic. The true scholastic is a mystical subtilizer. Out of logical atoms he builds his universe—he annihilates all living nature in order to put an artifice of thought in its place. His objective is an infinite automaton. Opposed to him is the raw intuitive thinker. He is a mystical macrologue. He hates rules and fixed forms. A wild violent life prevails in Nature— everything is alive. No laws—arbitrariness and miracles everywhere. He is purely dynamic.[4]

Novalis recognized both extremes and was fully cognizant of the dangers in each. While this cannot be said of all the Romantic poets, certainly Novalis and Goethe were not mere "raw intuitive thinkers." This is frequently a source of great error. While they revolted against the world as automaton, theirs was not an arbitrary world. In their mature thought we see them striving for a synthesis of these polar attitudes towards the world. The intellect which can grasp the fixed, created aspect of Nature (Coleridge's "Understanding")—while different from the power of Reason, the faculty whereby the creative principles themselves are beheld—was also given its full due. Herein lies the great question which each of these figures faced, at least unconsciously. What can be set forth in place of the New Philosophy promulgated through the Enlightenment which is not merely a "Romantic reaction"? For some the question remained unanswered. Novalis sought its answer in an intense study of Fichte's *Theory of the Sciences*, of mathematics, and of the technology of mining, studying at the renowned technical academy in Freiburg from 1797-99. Yet Novalis was unable to bring his reflections to a real completion. It remained for Goethe to develop an approach to Nature which is at once scientific and poetic. These two attitudes, usually thought completely antagonistic, became united in Goethe's scientific studies. Philosophy need not be cold, need not clip the wings of angels. Our own Emerson clearly recognized the positive import and challenge of science for the poet. He tells us, "[N]ever did any science originate, but by a poetic perception."[5]   The poet's sense of the harmony active within Nature need not be threatened by the results of science:

> And this undersong, this perfect harmony does not become less with more intimate knowledge of nature's laws but the analogy is felt to be deeper and more universal for every law that Davy or Cuvier or Laplace has revealed.

One senses in all these thinkers a like spirit striving for form and expression. That spirit tells us that the essential core of the scientific attitude is *not* inherently evil or destructive. Rather it is the misapplication of physical laws to the living—that is, to realms of Nature which go beyond simple mechanism—that is in error. It is our confusion of a mechanical thought-picture, or materialistic hypothesis, for Nature and its laws which destroys the living, moral Nature familiar to the Imagination of the poet. What is this Imagination and can it have a place in true science? Emerson characterizes it for us in his essay "The Poet":

> This insight, which expresses itself by what is called Imagination, is a very high sort of seeing, which does not come by study, but by the intellect being where and what it sees, by sharing the path or circuit of things through forms, and so making them translucid to others. The path of things is silent. Will they suffer a speaker to go with them? A spy they will not suffer; a lover, a poet, is the transcendency of their own nature—him they will suffer. This condition of true naming, on the poet's part, is his resigning himself to the divine aura which breathes through forms, and accompanying that.

It would be difficult to find a more beautiful description of what Goethe sought in his science. By careful and patient observation, the mind becomes "where and what it sees": it follows the gentle growth of a plant, the changing colors of the sky "by sharing the path or circuit of things through forms." This is an approach to Nature which, by being phenomenal, remains objective, while also allowing the living harmony within Nature to remain unaided by a superimposed mechanistic philosophy. In his observation of Nature, Goethe remained ever mindful of the higher unity which would reveal itself to his patient and developing soul. Thus the principle itself becomes experienced as Archetype through a "high sort of seeing." True naming is the poet's art. Or, in Steiner's words: "What appears in science as the Idea is in art the image."[6]

To discuss Goethe's science further would lead us too far afield. It has been done many times.[7] Our intention has been rather to place the struggles of Goethe and his colleagues with science in an historical perspective. In many ways we can see Goethe's scientific attempts as a turning point. The long descent of human experience from the divine into a deeper and deeper connection with the purely material culminated in the Enlightenment. Taken alone, its mechanistic philosophy imprisons the human being in "an artifice of thought ... an infinite automation." If rejected in its entirety, the world becomes wild, violent and arbitrary—purely dynamic. Goethe's significant contribution lies in his discovery of a manner of scientific inquiry which allows us to approach the spiritual within Nature and the human being. Imagine the joy of young Rudolf Steiner when the scientific basis for investigation of the spirit stood before him in Goethe's scientific studies, not as an abstract philosophy but as embodied in his botanical or color studies. Implicit within Goethe's scientific struggles dwelt a whole world conception which could act as the foundation for what would become anthroposophy. In Steiner, Goethean science was transformed into spiritual science, and the conscious ascent of the human being began.

Notes

1. Werner Heisenberg, *Across the Frontiers*, translated by P. Heath (San Francisco: Harper & Row, 1974).

2. Walter Heitler, *Der Berliner Germanistentag*, 1968 (Heidelberg, 1970). Translations by F. Amrine available on request.

3. Rudolf Steiner, *Goethe as Scientist*, translated by O. Wannamaker (Great Barrington, MA: Anthroposophic Press, 1950), 250.

4. Novalis, *Hymns to the Night and Other Selected Writings*, translated by C. Passage (Indianapolis, IN: Bobbs-Merrill, The Liberal Arts Press, 1960), 70.

5. P. Obuchowski, *The Relationship of Emerson's Interest in Science to his Thought*, Ph.D. thesis 1969 (70-4158) U. of Michigan, available from University Microfilms, Ann Arbor, MI.

6. Rudolf Steiner, *A Theory of Knowledge Based on Goethe's World Conception*, translated by O. Wannamaker (Great Barrington, MA: Anthroposophic Press, 1968), 117.

7. Arthur Zajonc, "Goethe's Theory of Color and Scientific Intuition," *American Journal of Physics*, vol. 44 (1977): 327-333 and "Facts as Theory: Aspects of Goethe's Philosophy of Science," *Goethe and the Sciences: A Reappraisal*, edited by F. Amrine, F.Zucker and H. Wheeler (Boston: Reidel, 1986).

Emerson's Epistemology with Glances at Rudolf Steiner

Gertrude Reif Hughes

As a teacher of literature, I've noticed in my students a hunger for Emerson's wisdom, but even more for his insistence on a creative, rather than a created, element in all human beings. No disillusionment can shake Emerson's faith in this element or obscure its freshness from his readers, whether he calls it Self, Over-Soul, Mind, Moral Sentiment, or God. The wise epigrams he is so famous for seem mere bumper stickers by comparison with his firm understanding that human beings are sources, not products.

When I was invited to give a paper at a session for Emerson scholars at the Modern Language Association's annual meeting this past Christmas (1985), I chose to connect Emerson to Rudolf Steiner through this feature of his thought. I chose this emphasis because the crucial thing to convey about Rudolf Steiner is that anthroposophy is not an orthodoxy but a mode of cognition. It seemed sensible, therefore, to connect Steiner and Emerson not through their wisdom, nor through their inspirational exhortations, but through their epistemology—the theory of knowledge and knowing that they share.

Steiner, of course, insisted that "spiritual science has no desire to lead to belief but to knowledge" ("The Nature of the Virgin Sophia and of the Holy Spirit," in the cycle on the Gospel of St. John, Hamburg, 1908; Steiner's italics). To most matter-based thinkers the very phrase "spiritual science" seems like a contradiction in terms, because such thinkers assume that empirical methods must be reserved for the physical while the non-physical, or spiritual, must be enshrined in a domain designated as "personal" and isolated from scientific scrutiny.

Both Steiner and Emerson see humans as sources of knowing rather than recorders of what is to be known. Both put this capacity to complete the world through thinking at the foundation of all their writings. Though Steiner is always more explicit and methodical than Emerson, both undeniably place at the very heart of what makes humans human the will-filled thinking that Science labored so hard to describe, defend, and introduce into culture. Both know intimately the paradox whereby it is our uniqueness that we all have in common and both based not only knowledge but a theory of knowing on this mystery. That's the affinity I try to describe in the paragraphs that follow.

In an 1837 journal entry, Emerson pondered a version of his favorite paradox, "the infinitude of the private man." Noting that many people feel dwarfed by circumstances, he recommended that they counter their melancholy by remembering their own infinitude. "As fast as you can," he urged, "break off your association with your personality and identify yourself with the Universe." Why does such self-transcendence make one both freer and more oneself, rather than less so? Because—and this is the paradox of "the infinitude of the private man"—"I could not be, but that absolute life circulated in me, and I could not think this without being that absolute life" (JMN V, 391).

Not only does "absolute life" confer individual existence upon him as it circulates in him, but, says Emerson, he can only have this perception because he himself is that absolute life. To repeat his words: "I could not be, but that absolute life circulated in me, and I could not think this without being that absolute life." These words reveal Emerson's affinity with Rudolf Steiner's philosophy of thinking. Emerson and Steiner share a radically self-referential epistemology in that both find in self-observation a starting point for reliable cognition. Each in his own way—Steiner more programmatically than Emerson—says that our own cognition is an activity which, when we ourselves observe it, reveals itself to be both objective and subjective. Our own act of thinking is unquestionably present for us to observe and as unquestionably it is our own activity, not something imposed upon us.

Thinking "is the unobserved element in our ordinary life of thought," says Rudolf Steiner in his *Philosophy of Freedom (1894; revised 1918)*. In that work and in his dissertation, *Truth and Knowledge* (1892), as well as in his 1920 lectures on Aquinas published as *The Redemption of*

Thinking, Steiner describes thinking as mainly a dynamic, creative activity, in contrast to Kant, who held that the main use of thinking is to portray the given, sensory world. Steiner says, "The primary reason for the existence of thinking is not that it should make pictures of the outer world, but that it should bring to full development being. That it portrays to us the outer world is a secondary process" (*Redemption*, p. 111). Like Emerson, Steiner seeks "original relation" (*Nature*, "Introduction"). He seeks a starting point for epistemology that neither assumes that the content of experience is as we perceive it, nor that it is always being falsified by thinking. The first position he calls naïve (or uncritical) realism; the second, naïve rationalism (*Truth and Knowledge* p. 332 and *passim*).

A proper starting point for a theory of knowledge must be neither objective, in the sense of ignoring a human knower, nor subjective, in the sense of being untrustworthy. It must be indubitable, yet pertain to the knower. In order to find a starting point for epistemology, Steiner wants to separate the directly given world picture from that which is derived by thinking. Of course, he says, we never consciously experience this directly given world picture, because we're always adding our consciousness and its contents. But we can take our world picture and *deduct* from it what we ourselves have added and thereby arrive, *in principle if not in fact*, at this directly given.

Before I continue, notice that Steiner, like Emerson, is not an idealist. Though sensory data cannot provide a starting point for epistemology, it's not because they are sensory, but because our thinking itself is uncritically mixed in with them, whereas the starting point for epistemology must be directly given, not just hypothesized or deduced to be directly given. In fact, Steiner gives an example of an error that many would say was a sensory error but that he shows is actually an error made by cognition, not by observation. The moon on the horizon appears larger than at the zenith. This, you say, is an error; the moon doesn't change size as it rises and sets, so my senses have deceived me. The error, however, is not in the observation—the moon does indeed appear larger in one position, smaller in the other. The error comes in the interpretation that this variable appearance of the moon means that the moon actually changed size. This is the error, and cognition makes it, not observation.

Though Steiner exposes the naïve rationalism of ascribing such an error to observation when it should be ascribed to interpretation, Steiner is not a naïve realist. He is not a logical positivist. Like Goethe, whose scientific works he edited as a young man, Steiner cherishes empiricism, but his great contribution is to identify thinking itself as an unrecognized field for observation. Indeed, the epistemological starting point which Steiner seeks, that about which thinking has made no prior claims or assumptions, turns out to be thinking itself. Steiner shows that ordinarily we fail to observe our own thinking; we take it for granted. In a sense, he says, it is granted; it is part of the given world picture. It differs, however, in this one respect: Whereas we cannot be immediately certain whether or not we produced the rest of the given world picture, with this one part of it that is our own thinking we can be sure that we ourselves produce it. True, people have hallucinations. They sometimes believe that what they are in fact making up has independent sensory existence. But about concepts and ideas we make no such mistake, Steiner says. "We do know absolutely directly that concepts and ideas appear only in the act of cognition and ... enter the sphere of the directly given" through this activity (*Truth and Knowledge*, 344). "A hallucination," he says "may appear as something externally given, but one would never take one's own concepts to be something given *without one's own thinking activity*" (*Truth and Knowledge*, 344; my emphasis). Our ideas, our concepts, then, come to us by our own activity of cognition. Our ideas we know we produce.

Notice the paradox; it is absolutely basic. Our cognition is part of the given because we can recognize it directly, that is, without having to draw any conclusions about it first. But (here is the paradox) what we directly know as given when we know our own cognition is this: that we produce it, that it is our own activity! Thus we ourselves produce this part of the given. The given contains an activity, cognition, and this activity, which we know to be our own act, produces concepts, including the concept: "There is a pre-cognitional given which is the starting point for cognition." To summarize: Cognition is both given and self-produced in that my self-production of it is what I directly know about it.

We are in the realm of paradox, but not necessarily in the solipsistic labyrinth that self-reflexivity conjures for many people (Hughes, 155-162). At least Emerson, like Steiner, would deny that self-reference disqualifies one's thought from validity. On the contrary, to learn to detect your own thinking and recognize that it is yours instead of excluding it from your scrutiny because it is yours—this skill Emerson exhorts his apprentice in self-reliance to practice:

> A man should learn to detect and watch that gleam of light which flashes across his mind from within, more than the lustre of the firmament of bards and sages. *Yet he dismisses without notice his thought, because it is his* ("Self-Reliance," paragraph one; my emphasis).

In other words, Emerson agrees with Steiner that "thinking is the unobserved element in our ordinary life of thought" (*The Philosophy of Freedom*, 61). Both Emerson and Steiner invite readers to observe their own thinking. Moreover, both relate the possibility of doing so to the possibility for freedom, the possibility for relying on no authority however illustrious, but only on oneself. This relationship between cognition and self-reliance or freedom is the goal of Steiner's epistemology, and the deepest impetus for Emerson's interest in the "original relation" that he calls for in his first book and is trying to cultivate twenty-five years later in the *Conduct of Life*.

In closing, let me develop a connection between Emerson's demand for "original relation" in the Introduction to *Nature* and his worship of the Beautiful Necessity in "Fate," the keynote essay of *The Conduct of Life*. As you will see, both these concepts involve the kind of radically self-critical relation between knower and known that Steiner's epistemology calls for. If you ignore this epistemological ground, Emerson's discourse sounds merely oratorical; but if you credit the demand for self-knowing cognition that underlies Emerson's concepts of "original relation" and "Beautiful Necessity," then his rhapsodies become activating insights, as he intended.

"Why should not we also enjoy an original relation to the universe?"

Emerson challenges. "Let us demand our own works and laws and worship—our own connection to the world, not some inherited or derived one." In calling for "original relation," Emerson required for each single person a completely individual starting point for cognition, one undistorted—and also unaided—by others' assumptions or conclusions. Such a demand requires much *from* its beneficiaries as well as *for* them. Like Steiner's starting point for epistemology, Emerson's "original relation" could only *make* free an individual who knew how, or practiced how, to *be* free.

The most austere form of original relation is the relation between individual and circumstance called Fate—"the tie between person and event," Emerson styled it in his essay on the subject (W, VI, 30). Musing on the "tie between person and event," Emerson calls it "the secret of the world" and urges his audience to penetrate that secret tie so that they can learn to see that they and their circumstances are not two but one: "A man will see his character emitted in the events that seem to meet [him], but which [actually] exude from and accompany him" (W, VI, 42). When you achieve this insight, Emerson knows, you transform something alien and limiting into something known and supporting; you recognize your circumstance as your Self, your fate as your destiny.

This relationship between yourself and your world is original indeed! It's entirely yours, can belong to none other. Yes, it is dire and austere to equate that heady "original relation" Emerson is calling for in *Nature* with the "Beautiful Necessity" which he worships at the end of "Fate." But Emerson's optimism demands much, because it promises much— nothing less than each individual's identity with the "absolute life" which, he said, both constitutes each one of us and connects each to all the rest of the world. In this identity between each and all, Emerson finds epistemological ground for radical transvaluations like the equation of "original relation" with Beautiful Necessity. By showing that he shares this ground with Rudolf Steiner, I've tried to highlight how both Emerson and Steiner unsettle dualistic habits of mind and challenge some danger- ously limiting perceptions and values that these habits sponsor.

List of Works Cited

Emerson, Ralph Waldo *The Complete Works of Ralph Waldo Emerson*, Centenary Edition. 12 vols. Boston and New York: Houghton Mifflin and Co., 1903-1904. Cited as W, followed by volume number and page.

_____, *Nature*. Any edition.

_____, "Self-Reliance." Any edition.

_____, *The Journals and Miscellaneous Notebooks of Ralph Waldo Emerson*, ed.

William H. Gilman et alia. 14 vols. Cambridge Harvard University Press, 1960–, cited as JMN, followed by volume number and page.

Hughes, Gertrude Reif, *Emerson's Demanding Optimism*. Baton Rouge: Louisiana State University Press, 1984.

Steiner, Rudolf, *The Philosophy of Freedom* and *Truth and Knowledge*, ed. Paul M. Allen, trans. Rita Stebbing. West Nyack, New York: Rudolf Steiner Publications, Inc., 1963. (NB: The two titles are bound together as one book in this edition.)

_____, *The Redemption of Thinking: A Study in the Philosophy of Thomas Aquinas*, trans. and ed. A.P. Shepherd and Mildred Robertson Nicoll. Spring Valley, New York: Anthroposophic Press, 1983 (second printing).

Emerson's Demanding Optimism

John Wulsin

Emerson's Demanding Optimism by Gertrude Reif Hughes (Baton Rouge, LA: Louisiana State University Press, 1984), 170 pages.

Gertrude Reif Hughes has written *Emerson's Demanding Optimism*, shedding fine light on one of America's seminal minds. Hard to begin in July, better read in September, her book will enable its readers to read Emerson more actively any time of the year. Writing with both the breadth of knowledge of a mature scholar and the intensity of a keen thinker, Gertrude Hughes soon finds her voice and guides us into a soberly exhilarating disclosure of the way Emerson's mind works. The way it works. This book is no tour through the library of Emerson's ideas. If anything, we join Emerson in his mental laboratory. The book is a labor; it is a call to labor. It is an endeavor even to recreate in the mind of the reader the kind of activity which Hughes energetically discerns to be the nature of Emerson's mind, not simply in one essay, nor in one stage of his life, but throughout the course of his maturing thinking.

Emerson's Demanding Optimism establishes early a fundamental, explicit precept behind Emerson's writings—"recall that Emerson's essays are designed to empower rather to instruct. ... What perception as a concept does for an Emersonian argument, perception as a capacity does for the Emersonian reader. It throws him on the party of the eternal; that is, it renders him of the maker not the made." Readers of this journal may be surprised to find in such a public, scholarly book a reference to Steiner's *Knowledge of the Higher Worlds and Its Attainment* as "...the best book I know of concerning the kind of thinking Emerson alludes to in 'Wealth' and the kind of perception all his sums and solutions call for."

Readers of this journal may be less surprised than the scholarly world at the fundamental, implicit precept which Gertrude Hughes has brilliantly discerned in Emerson's thinking. "How can I follow his train of thought?" and "He seems to be going in circles" are common concerns of struggling readers of Emerson. Hughes sees that Emerson's coherence is not one of fluency nor of sequential architectural construct. "Rather, this coherence is that of a gathering, a community. ...Emerson's technique is not to draw a line, nor even to cultivate a growth. ...His technique is to create a firmament and then populate it." Her distillation of the essential formative principle in Emerson's writings and in her own book is that "Emerson's beginnings are climactic and his endings initiative."

In fact, it may well be that no one has ever read a book like *Emerson's Demanding Optimism*, for I doubt if any critical work like it has been written. Gertrude Reif Hughes begins with one of Emerson's last books, *The Conduct of Life*, and then proceeds backwards through major works of his adult life, culminating with his first publication *Nature*, written when he was thirty-three. Those already familiar with Emerson are likely to discover an astonishing power in the experience of being led from thoughts at the end of his life back home finally to many of the conclusions of his first works. Those less familiar with Emerson will learn ways to read him that no one has taught before. And the scholarly world just could be revolutionized by Hughes' approach and how it reveals Emerson's mind.

Parents and teachers especially will be interested in one aspect of Emerson's thinking. People have spoken before of how dramatically, like Plato, Emerson explores thoughts. In an essay several voices express different relationships to an idea. In that context Gertrude Hughes pays special attention to Emerson's fable-making tendency, an unusually malleable capacity to create a fable appropriate for the moment, drawing from the present or the past. An example of Emerson's drawing from local resources is an anecdote he shared in his address at Thoreau's funeral. A friend had said, "I love Henry, but I cannot like him; and as for taking his arm, I should as soon think of taking the arm of an elm tree." It emerged in later years that Emerson himself was that friend, fabling his own words to make them serve a context appropriately. Another example Hughes mentions occurs in his essay "Character" as he has been discussing the presence of a man of character. Emerson suddenly shifts, *in medias res*, into an original fable, by reporting the following conversation:

> "O Iole! How did you know Hercules was a god?" "Because," answered Iole, "I was content the moment my eyes fell on him. When I beheld Theseus, I desired that I might see him offer battle, or at least guide his horses in the chariot-race; but Hercules did not wait for a contest; he conquered whether he stood, or walked, or sat, or whatever thing he did."

Classical allusions aside, the fable is Emerson's own. It is an example of a mobility of mind which reading Emerson will generate in us, as we attempt to meet a child's or peer's wound or misdeed, whether of body or soul, in a way appropriate to the moment.

Perhaps most revealing of the quality of *Emerson's Demanding Optimism* is the way Hughes' own mind works. The most distinctive quality of her approach has already been mentioned, working through Emerson's thoughts from the end to the beginning of his mature thinking life. In the process Hughes exercises again and again a keen grasp of polarity in thought and in language, a capacity making her especially suited to illuminate Emerson, whose thinking is so polar. Aware of the danger that examples will appear incomprehensible out of context, I mention several anyway, just to show how she works with language:

> To begin with fate and end with illusions is to begin with the deceptively implacable and to end with the implacably deceptive. (p. 27)

> Reality is the post-surfaces counterpart of forgetfulness; subjectiveness is the post-surfaces counterpart of temperament. (p. 480)

> But it is the right to speak that Emerson seems to be disclaiming, rather than the rightness of what is being spoken. (p. 64)

> For him the truth is not tested by the instance; the instance is salvaged or translated—or, to use his term, made transparent—by the truth. His is not a quest for the certainty required by a hypothesis, but for the vigor required by a certainty. ... (p. 100)

Quite wakeful and discerning, she can be even more microscopically attentive to Emerson's language itself:

> "Immortal, necessary, uncreated." Though it is implicit and adjectival rather than explicit and nominalized, this grouping of epithets constitutes a definition of ideas (or the ME) as clearly as Emerson's famous sentence about the NOT-ME constitutes a definition of nature. (p. 138)

As well, she is capable of large distinctions not so commonly clear:

> In reassessing motivation, Emerson seeks to reconcile his spiritual conviction that motive is the mystery of conduct with his psychological observation that intention is far from insuring achievement or giving it worth. (p. 115)

In short, Gertrude Reif Hughes serves her subject well.

Whether she will find an audience beyond scholars remains a question. I deeply hope so, for her concerns are not simply scholarly but profoundly human; they address not just thinkers; but Emerson's Man Thinking. By working back through Emerson's thinking she guides her readers through the experience of the deeply empowering, not weakening, character of Emerson's optimism.

Novalis and the Easter Thought

Christopher Bamford

> *I say to everyone—He lives!*
> *And has arisen from death,*
> *That He is present in our midst*
> *And ever gives us breath.*
>
> — Novalis, *Sacred Songs*

> *The whole of our western culture needs the Easter thought, needs, in other words, to be lifted to the Spirit. ... Easter must become an inner festival, a festival in which we celebrate in ourselves the victory of the Spirit over the body. ... When enough human beings realize that the Spirit must come to life again in modern civilization, the World-Easter thought will become a reality. ...*
>
> — Rudolf Steiner, *Spirit Triumphant*

The Spirit must come to life! The Easter thought, which our time needs so profoundly, is that in which Novalis lives. In his life the veil of appearances is lifted, and we see the spiritual at work in history and hear the victory of the Spirit proclaimed.

For Novalis, light itself, whose manifold transformations create physical reality, was only a shadow of a divine-spiritual light, awaiting human consciousness for its release and its fulfillment. In him the living knowledge was reborn that, since Golgotha, human beings and the earth were once again united with the cosmos and that all things were infused with the Spirit of the Resurrection, wanting only human sacrificial action for their restoration.

Novalis was born in 1772, as Friedrich von Hardenberg, into an austere, puritanical, Pietistic household which, governed by a precise routine, revolved around devotions and bible lessons.

Until his ninth year the poet was dreamy, backward and slow to learn. Then came a crisis—dysentery—and months of sickness, with death expected daily. But he revived and with the cure manifested a remarkable mental awakening, demonstrating great gifts of memory, attention and observation. Soon he outgrew the tutors that the neighborhood was able to provide, and in order to remedy this and, at the same time, to strengthen his faith, his father sent him away to the founding Pietistic community of Neudietendorf.

Friedrich went, but resisted inwardly. A new sense of individuality was coming to light within him. This was strengthened by the next turn of events, for his uncle—a bachelor and man of the world, a Knight of the German Order of Knighthood—had heard of his nephew's predicament and offered to help. Friedrich thus found himself thrust suddenly into the midst of the worldly and skeptical rationalist culture of the Enlightenment.

For the next years—from age twelve to eighteen—Friedrich lived in this polarity of Pietistic father and Enlightenment uncle. Then, at eighteen, he went to Jena, where he studied history and philosophy under the poet Schiller. Next, he moved to Leipzig, where he met the Schlegels, founders of German romanticism. Finally, he went to Wittenberg, where Luther had nailed his Theses. Here, in 1795, at the age of twenty-three, he matriculated.

By now he had written and published some poems, and had read and discussed a great deal. But apart from his personal appearance, which was gentle, innocent, luminous and transparent, suggesting to Friedrich Schlegel the features of St. John the Evangelist as portrayed by Dürer— apart, that is, from who he was—there was nothing yet about him of Novalis. He was still Friedrich von Hardenberg, a brilliant and somewhat scattered young man, who had not yet found his direction. But the seed of that direction had already been sown.

On October 25, 1794, Friedrich was appointed law clerk in Tennstedt. On November 17 of that year, on a journey to collect taxes, he who was to write, "We dream of journeys through the universe, but is not the universe within us?" saw Sophia von Kühn for the first time.

Within a quarter of an hour, his mind was made up. Sensing "affinities closer than blood," he saw in this young girl, not yet thirteen years of age, "the immortal idea of being a man." Something in him then began the painful process of awakening. This is one of the great mysteries. Sophia was to become for him the vehicle of unity, of resurrection, of life itself, and yet she was only an unlettered schoolchild.

Who or what was she? In his introduction to the *Works of Novalis*, Tieck wrote: "No description can express in what grace and celestial harmony the fair being moved, what beauty shone in her, what softness and majesty encircled her." Goethe, too, was moved by her.

For Friedrich himself she was "one of the noblest, most ideal figures ever to walk the earth." And yet the portrait in his diary is of a completely human and thoroughly natural mixture of qualities. The only suggestion of something different enters in a strange phrase in which he notes: "Sophia does not wish to be anybody for she is somebody."

On her thirteenth birthday, on March 21, 1795, Friedrich and Sophia became engaged. In his betrothal ring, Friedrich inscribed: *May Sophia become my guardian angel.*

Then, in autumn of that year, Sophia fell ill. Her sickness came in painful waves; she suffered agonies; and in the measure that Sophia suffered and physically wasted away, Friedrich's love and devotion increased. Finally, two days before her fifteenth birthday, on March 19, 1797, Sophia died. Friedrich was twenty-five. Then on Good Friday of the same year came the death of his dear brother, Erasmus.

Thus death surrounded Friedrich and became, as it were, the womb out of which the great transformation would occur. Through the death of Sophia and his continuing, perpetually expanding love for her, the process of his rebirth in the Spirit began. He wrote to Schlegel: "My love has become a flame that consumes all that is earthly. ... There are within my soul more powers of healing, of endurance, of resistance, than I had known." To Woltmann, he wrote: "I am wholly content. I have gained anew the power that rises over death. My being has taken on unity and form. Even now a new life is burgeoning within me."

Distraught with grief, torn apart with pain, Friedrich had begun to seek Sophia within himself. Turning aside from the bright luminous world of the senses, he began to discover the "holy, ineffable, mysterious Night" within. Overcome with profound sadness, gradually he had begun to sense a "precious balm" and, feeling the heavy wings of his soul uplifted, he discovered a new soul-world within, one whose wonders far outweighed those of the day-world without. Here he felt for the first time truly human, and, moved beyond anything he had ever known before, he offered himself up to the Dark Queen of the Night, whose "dominion is timeless and spaceless and where the secret sacrifice of love burns eternally."

Friedrich began to visit Sophia's grave, going for the first time on Easter Morning. Less than a month later, it occurred: "In the evening I visited Sophia. I was indescribably happy there. There were flashes of ecstasy. I wafted the grave from me as though it were dust. Centuries passed in a flash. Her presence was tangible. I felt she might appear at any moment." In the *Hymns to the Night*, he puts it thus: "All at once the bond of birth broke the Light's fetters. ... The region rose gently aloft and over this region hovered my released and new-born spirit. The mound became a cloud of dust and through the cloud I beheld the transfigured features of my beloved. Now I knew when the final morning will be: when Light no longer frightens away Night and Love, and slumber shall be eternal and only an inexhaustible dream." In other words, when the tyranny of mere sense perception is overcome and sense reality no longer frightens away supersensible knowledge, reality is transformed into a continuous vision of creative imagination. With this experience, Novalis was born— metamorphosed from Friedrich von Hardenberg. In his diary entry for June 30, he simply notes: "Christ and Sophia."

Renewed in this way, Novalis returned to life with vigor and purpose. He moved to Freiburg to study mining and technology, and, reading deeply in alchemy, Plotinus, Boehme, he began to write and publish. Indeed, as though the transformation that he was undergoing could be transferred, in fact had to be transferred, to everything, Novalis now conceived the dream of making everything new, of renewing all science, art and religion. This project he called Romanticism. "The world must be romanticized," he wrote. "In this way one discovers its original meaning. Romanticizing is nothing but a qualitative raising to a higher power. ... The lower self becomes identified with the higher." This is the Easter thought.

Through such "magic idealism," sense reality was to be continually informed by supersensible knowledge, poetry was to be "philosophized," religion and science "poeticized," until, humanity becoming all in all, paradise was regenerated. Poetry here is to be understood as "practical religion," religion as "practical poetry," both overcoming the oppositions between the world and mind, nature and the cosmos, humanity and God. This poetry, then, is creative of the whole person.

As Novalis wrote of the Sage in "The Apprentices of Sais": "He looked for analogies in all things—conjunctures, correspondences, till he could no longer see anything in isolation. All the perceptions of his senses crowded into great variegated images: he heard, saw, touched and thought simultaneously. He loved to bring strangers together. Now stars were men to him, now men stars, stones were animals, clouds were plants; he played with powers and phenomena, he knew just where to find this shape or the other, to make them appear."

We must not forget, however, that it is Sophia alone who makes this vision possible. Indeed, since his experience at her tomb, Novalis wrote that he had begun to perceive—to dream, to know—"in" and "through" Sophia, that she had become for him an organ and a realm of true cognition.

It is as though, through the physical death of Sophia, through the physical separation from her that made him seek her within himself, Novalis underwent a great purification in which all that was impure in his love for Sophia was burned away. Through her death, he seems to have experienced the death of all that was petty, possessive, material, impenetrable and earthbound in himself; through pure selfless grief he was able to let himself die into her. Thus, at the graveside, it was as though he were turned inside out, so that what was within, crossing, came without and simultaneously what was without came within, crossing again. Commentators have said that he arrived at the point where subject and object were indistinguishable. It is perhaps truer to say, however, that purified within and turned about, the outer became transparent, directly permeable by thought and was revealed as the accomplished work of the Gods now accessible within:

> He reached the goal at Sais; he lifted the veil of the Goddess, only to see, wonder of wonders—himself.

From this experience then, Novalis could see that the cosmos and nature, turned into a corpse by materialistic science, was capable of resurrection and that this resurrection depended upon human activity and cooperation, that, in his words: "Humanity is the higher sense of the planet, the nerve that binds the planet to the upper world, the eye that raises it to heaven." Thus Novalis knew that "We are on a mission. We are called for the fashioning of the earth." And he knew, too, that the goal of this, as in St. John's teaching, is love. "Love is the ultimate goal of the world's history," he wrote, "the Amen of the universe. The heart is the key to the world and to life. ... From this point of view, Christ is the Key to the World."

This Christ is not primarily the Crucified One, nor the King, nor the Teacher, but rather that Spirit Who, since Golgotha, in the words of Friedrich Benesch, permeates and fills the "in-between," the crossing points, the boundaries and differences between things. "The Throne of the Soul," runs a fragment, "is there where interior and exterior fuse. There is fusion at every point of their interpenetration." It is as though Novalis' participation in Sophia's death, and the purification this wrought within him, turned him inside out, Christ arose at the crossing over of inside and outside, just as he arose at the crossing over of past and future Golgotha:

> Suddenly, as though from Heaven
> From the grave the stone was riven,
> And my soul was opened wide.
>
> Who appeared, my life restoring,
> Ask not, nor who knelt adoring ...

This impulse of resurrection we may experience as the guiding center of all that Novalis did. It is the unifying element, the heart of his teaching. In his essay, *Christendom or Europe*, for instance, the theme is "history as gospel": history as the bearer of the Good News. Novalis composed it in the autumn of 1799; he read it in Jena in November, a year and a half before he died. It met with tremendous resistance from his contemporaries, who were not yet ready for it. It was even omitted from the first edition of his collected writings. One can see why.

Novalis begins with an idealized picture of primitive, almost primordial Christianity, of a timeless Church based upon "childlike faith in Christ," His vicar on earth (the Pope), His Divine Mother, and the Communion of Saints. Everywhere the Gospel of Life was preached, everyone sought to make the Kingdom of Heaven the only kingdom on earth. But this was a "first love." It "died away amid the press of business life." Wars, schisms proliferated. Protestantism arose, a true impulse, but one diverted from its truth. Dividing the invisible Church, shattering the dream of a universal Christian community, it fragmented Europe into nationalisms.

For Novalis, Luther himself is the chief offender. Misjudging the spirit of Christianity, he introduced the idolatry of the "letter," and so forgot the worship and the wisdom of the "spirit." Forgetting the esotericism of the Bible, he substituted for it "a different, highly alien, worldly science, philosophy." Hatred of religion, of the spirit, of imagination and emotion was the consequence. Poetry was shorn from nature. Every trace of the Holy was obliterated. "The infinite creative music of the universe" was reduced "to the monotonous clatter of a monstrous mill."

Chaos and anarchy followed. But in this—between the horns of misguided religion and misguided philosophy—Novalis sensed the possibility of a reconciling agent, "a third element, which is at once secular and superworldly." Until the great *agápe*—which would be brought about by the religion, by joy and "faith in the universal capacity of all earthly things to be the bread and wine of eternal life"—wars would continue. But the presence of the dream of reconciliation foretold its future. Novalis foresaw: "a new Golden Age, with dark and infinite eyes, an age prophetic, wonder-working, miraculously healing, comforting and kindling eternal life—a great age of reconciliation, a Savior who, like a good spirit, is at home among men, believed in though not seen, visible under countless forms to believers, consumed as bread and wine, embraced as a bride, breathed as air, heard as word and song."

Thus Novalis, together with that tremendous company of souls known as the Romantics, is a prophet for a new era of peace and harmony, a new culture in which science, art and religion rise again in unity and work through humankind for the transformation of the earth.

Like all prophets, Novalis was not so much of his own time as of a future only he could foresee. When he died, his friend Tieck edited an edition of the available collected works. Many papers, however, remained unknown to the public. Then in 1930, the descendants of the poet offered a large collection of manuscripts for auction. The publisher Shocken bought them; but the war intervened before they could be published, and it was not until 1968 that they finally saw the light of day. These papers, it now turns out, contained over 2,000 fragments and constituted the notes or groundwork for Novalis' *Totalwissenschaft* or Encyclopedia. Those who have studied them say that his thought as manifested in these notes was not only remarkable in his time, but so far in advance of it that even we cannot yet understand it.

In this sense, Novalis is a teacher for the future. "When artists will be pious and love Christ like Novalis," wrote Schleiermacher, "then will the great resurrection be celebrated."

Yeats, The Rosicrucians and Rudolf Steiner

Andrew J. Welburn

PART I

Yeats' poetry enjoys widespread popularity these days, and by no means only among formal students of literature. Many people recognize the power of his writing, though they may find him sometimes "difficult." He speaks in the tones of his great Romantic predecessors, Blake and Shelley. But he is also recognizably modern, and his words seem to engage the modern world. Indeed he seems able to invest with a spiritual significance the immediate events of his time and ours.

We are aware, as we read, of a man who, despite his bardic persona, is engagingly human, who has his failings and frustrations, sometimes to a distressing extent. Over half his long life was given to the hopeless love of a woman who decisively rejected him several times: Maud Gonne, herself almost a mythical figure in the painful story of the birth of the Irish state. For Yeats, she was a dream from which he could not awake, at least before her marriage to a man who was everything he was not: a soldier and man of unselfconscious action. Yet she was not Yeats' only door into what he called "The Land of Heart's Desire," or aspiration for a world of imaginative fulfillment beyond that of ordinary consciousness. Not many of Yeats' readers know that he was a student of esoteric wisdom. In the beginning, that too was little more than a dream, perhaps enabling the younger Yeats to write misty and evocative verse with an aura of the supernatural. But whereas Maud Gonne was to prove a destructive and bitter dream, Yeats' interest in esotericism was a dream that, as he later put it, could be expanded to include reality.

The deepening and maturing of Yeats' occultism is the theme I wish to follow through his life and work. The story reaches its crisis, as regards both Yeats' earthly and his spiritual love, in connection with Rudolf

Steiner. Indeed, I shall suggest that Steiner provides much more of a key to Yeats' later development than has previously been thought.[1] We must begin, however, with the days of Yeats' dreaming.

As a child, he would often wander off from his friends, lie down, and dream. His sleeping mind was full of images, though when he left school he still thought, like his father, to turn them into paintings rather than poems. It was at the Dublin Art School that he met George Russell (better known from the pseudonym AE, which he soon adopted to sign his mystical verse), the man who helped him discover his twin vocations of magic and poetry. Together they founded the Dublin Hermetic Society, a small group of vague seekers whom Yeats afterwards recalled with some amusement, interested in everything from poetry to the fourth dimension. In their company Yeats encountered the teachings of Theosophy, an oriental teaching brought to the West by H.P. Blavatsky who had spent some time in Tibet and claimed to have learnt there the "secret doctrine" behind Buddhism—and, as it turned out, behind all the other world religions too.

Theosophy offered a comprehensive "alternative" view of such matters as evolution, the nature of matter, the destiny of man, and was by no means without strong ideas once one had managed to wade one's way into Blavatsky's style. Claude Wright, one of the Hermetic Society members who became a lifelong theosophist, was dispatched to visit her in London in 1885; but she told him, "Go back to your native Dublin and found a lodge there." Her judgment turned out to be perspicacious, since the founding of the Theosophical Society's Dublin Lodge, according to E. Boyd in his study of *Ireland's Literary Renaissance*, was comparable in importance for the Irish movement with the publication of O'Grady's *History of Ireland*, "the two events being complementary to any complete understanding of the literature of the Revival."[2] At around this time, too, Yeats was beginning to realize that the struggle to find a consciousness beyond one's mere personality had a meaning in the splintered country of Ireland beyond the vague curiosities of the Dublin Hermetic students—a nationalist and Celtic meaning. It is interesting that Steiner's exploration of the "consciousness-soul" stressed the historical role of England in its unfolding. The objectivism of Bacon, the "passive-mind" philosophies of Locke and Hume, the mechanical universe of Newton: these are symptoms of a deeply rooted English mode of consciousness, at once a source of power over the world yet also the origin of denials and shortcomings. There was an obvious danger that Yeats' struggle against materialism might simply merge into his dream of the Celtic past, becoming a war against Saxon intellectualism. Others belonging to "the Celtic Twilight" were to identify the wisdom of the Druids with that of the Eastern sages and theosophy, and urge a retreat into a luminous mythical past. But Yeats resisted too simple an alliance.

The year 1887 took him instead to the heart of the spiritual enemy, to London. He soon took advantage of his proximity to the Theosophical headquarters and met Madame Blavatsky. He wrote later that "she made upon me an impression of generosity and indulgence." She extended both to Yeats, and when in 1888 she founded the Esoteric Section for those pupils desiring deeper instruction, he was rapidly made a member. Unfortunately, Yeats proved so distracting that in less than two years he was asked to leave. The fact was that the theosophical pageant of the universe, with its cycles within cycles, its elusive superhuman Masters somewhere in Tibet, proved crucially unable to satisfy all of Yeats' demands. A part of him wanted a truth he could test in action, in changing the world, in challenging his fellow human beings. The Eastern aspiration of the Theosophists to a contemplation of things ultimately so quiescent that it became mystical oneness-and-nothingness (*nirvana*) led in quite the opposite direction.

The blow of departure was not great. For Yeats was already starting to find his way into a more congenial, though hardly any less esoteric, society. The Hermetic Students of the Golden Dawn were an association of aspirants to knowledge of the occult who based their approach on the traditional Western doctrines of Hermetic *gnosis*, the Christianized *kabbalah*, and Renaissance alchemy. In common with the Freemasons, to whom they were in some ways related, they had also absorbed something of the fascination with Egyptian Mysteries that was especially widespread at that time of archeological and textual discoveries. Most of their Egyptian profundities were learnt, however, in places no more obscure than the British Museum and its famous Reading Room.

The esoteric practices they undertook are usually described in books as "magic," which is correct so far as it goes but can give a misleading impression. With the exception of spectacular deviants like Aleister Crowley, who quickly left the Order, they were not interested in supernatural trickery. Their magic was of the type known as "theurgy," which uses magical techniques for the purpose of bringing the aspirant into touch with the Divine—whether in himself, as his "Guardian Angel," or on higher cosmic levels of existence. Work toward the divine goal was as intensive and demanding, and more "practical" than in the Esoteric Section.

The Order of the Golden Dawn was organized on the analogy of the ancient Mysteries, notably those of Eleusis in classical Greece. Thus each of its "Temples" had a Hierophant, Hiereus (priest), Hegemon (leader), Kerux (herald), Dadouchos (torch-bearer), etc. There were various stages of ritual initiation, in the course of which the esoteric symbolism gradually unfolded its meaning and awoke powers in the depths of the soul. Prominent in the symbolism are references to light, described by Israel Regardie (who has published the Golden Dawn rituals and so brought them, as it were, exoterically into the light of the day) as the central idea of the Golden Dawn.

> Thus, when the Hierophant leaves the throne of the East, he represents the Higher Self in action, and as Osiris he marks the active descent of the supernal splendor. For he utters, while leaving the dais with wand uplifted, "I come in the power of the Light; I come in the Light of Wisdom. I come in the Mercy of the Light. The Light hath healing in its wings." And having brought the Light to the aspirant, he retires to his throne, as though that divine Genius of whom he is the Temple symbol and agent awaited the deliberate willing return of the aspirant himself to the everlasting abode of the Light. [3]

The archaic mystery of illumination has been enriched in their rites by the mysticism of the kaballah, which inspired Milton's "Hail Holy Light"; by the rediscovered Egyptian Book of the Dead or "Chapters of Coming Forth by Day"; as well as by the Gnostic-Hermetic concept of the "man of light," the inner man waiting to be discovered and revealed within us. Important for Yeats, too, were the meditations on colours and forms which seem on occasion to have fed directly into his poetry.

Initiation led through various "grades." The structure for these derived from a strange manuscript—written in cypher and containing "summary notes of Ceremonies"—whose provenance no one appears to have satisfactorily explained. The grades it names, however, correspond to those of a Masonic association known in Germany in the eighteenth century, called the Order of the Gold and Rosy Cross (*Gold and Rosenkreuzer Orden*)—so that some connection with the so-called High Grade Masonry and its rites, and perhaps with Germany, seems certain. These grades had also been adopted by the Societas Rosicruciana in Anglia, or Rosicrucian Society of England, a society of High Grade Masons founded in 1866 to which all the founders and earliest prominent members of the Golden Dawn belonged. Maud Gonne, whom Yeats introduced to the Order, left it after getting a whiff of its Masonic connections. She believed, probably correctly, that the Freemasons were working in northern Ireland for union with England; she was certainly wrong about the Golden Dawn, however, which was permeated by the Celtic enthusiasm of S.L. Mathers—MacGregor Mathers he liked to call himself—and of his wife Mina or Moina Bergson, sister of the well-known philosopher.

The origins of the Order of the Golden Dawn were more obscured than clarified by the official information given to neophytes. The "Historic Lecture" invested the Order with an atmosphere of grandiose antiquity, and more or less asserted that many of the famous seers and mystics of the past had been members, although nobody before Yeats thought of adding the unlikely name of William Blake to the list. In fact, the Order had been founded no earlier than 1888. But the mythology of its past was perhaps what Yeats called, in another context, "a necessary extravagance" and hardly affected the serious content of its teaching. Whether its three founders MacGregor Mathers, a coroner named Wynn Westcott and a certain Dr. W.R. Woodman had any idea of the sources of the Cypher manuscript and its rituals, or the origins of its Rosicrucian symbolic teaching, seems more than uncertain. There was some talk about a German adept called Fräulein Sprengel who had been in touch at the time of the foundation; later she was to be confused with the Fräulein Alice Sprengel who acted the part of Theodora in the first production of *Die Pforte der Einweihung*. But she, too, may have been an "extravagance," since all attempts to trace her subsequently drew a blank. Yeats recalled in his *Autobiographies* how he met Mathers in the British Museum, prior to his initiation in 1887.

> At the British Museum Reading Room I often saw a man of thirty-six, or thirty-seven, in a brown velveteen coat, with a gaunt

resolute face, and an athletic body, who seemed, before I heard his name, or knew the nature of his studies, a figure of romance.

At this stage Yeats was decidedly impressed.

He had copied many manuscripts on magic ceremonial and doctrine in the British Museum, and was to copy many more in Continental libraries, and it was through him mainly that I began certain studies and experiences, that were to convince me that images well up before the mind's eye from a deeper source than conscious or subconscious memory.

In the light of subsequent difficulties, it was MacGregor Mathers whom Yeats described as the "necessary extravagance," at a time of inner crisis for the Order. The Cypher manuscript had given grades and rituals for no more than the first five stages, the outer shell of initiation. Beyond the Order of the Golden Dawn in the Outer, to give it its full title, lay the true heart of the organization, an order within an order, the college of adepts who made up the Order of the Rose of Ruby and the Cross of Gold. But the content of the Cypher manuscript ran out at the point of transition, and it was by no means clear that anyone in the Order, including its three founder chiefs, was in a position to supply what it lacked. Mathers, undoubtedly the most "magically advanced" of them all, provided a Portal, or introductory rite, to the Second Order. He also began to elaborate the syllabus for its lowest rung (Adeptus Minor), throwing in a vast amount of his occult learning, and was still tinkering at it when the problems that were to split the Golden Dawn irremediably and lead to its disappearance from history sprang up around him. These difficulties have a certain bearing on our story, because when the crisis came, Yeats played an unexpectedly important role.

Whatever may have been the source of the Golden Dawn teachers, they were of a nature to assist Yeats far more in his imaginative development than were the doctrines of esoteric theosophy. The latter were oriented toward a transcendent, unfathomable God hidden behind the maze of cyclic manifestations. The Golden Dawn teachings were Rosicrucian, both in the sense that they embodied the Christianizing of the occult tradition which had been undertaken by the Rosicrucians of the seventeenth century, and in their attitude to the world and man. Its adepts did not aspire to Himalayan retreats, but felt themselves to be a part of significant world happenings. MacGregor Mathers foresaw terrible wars in the twentieth century and desperate struggles to bring about fraternity and mutual love as the basis of a new society; at least the first part of his prophecy proved true. The initiate of the Golden Dawn aimed to be a decisive personality, actively concerned with and working in the world. The actress Florence Farr (later Florence Emery) expressed this Rosicrucian character of their ideal as the decision of the adept "to choose a life that shall bring him in touch with the sorrows of his race rather than accept the nirvana open to him." Yeats himself struggled to describe the character of his Golden Dawn meditation, which he said was an attempt "to lay hands upon some dynamic and substantializing force as distinguished from the Eastern quiescent and supersensualizing state of the soul movement downwards upon life not upwards out of life."

Such a movement of imagination might find its images in the religion of the Incarnation, and the trials of initiation might find their archetype in the sufferings and life-giving death of a Savior on the cross, one who chose to share the sorrows of his race. Richard Ellman has stressed the Christian character of the Golden Dawn, especially in the higher grades. The importance of the annual Corpus Christi celebrations also points the same way. By 1893, points out Ellmann, Yeats had reached the higher grades: "In that year he attained the inner order of the Golden Dawn and, in the initiation of the Path of the Portal, he lay down in the tomb, died a symbolic death, and rose reborn in spirit, Christified."[4]   Nevertheless, Yeats' relationship to Christianity remained a difficult one, though it is no denial of his fundamental beliefs that he felt the need to "unite the radical truths of Christianity to those of a more ancient world." For he felt that Christianity had lost touch with much in the soul life of the people and he was thinking no doubt of the Irish people in the course of its checkered history. And indeed in that he may have been right.

At any rate, Yeats was sure about the value of his occult studies in their Rosicrucian form for his writing of verse. He wrote to John O'Leary, the prominent Irish nationalist:

> Now as to Magic. It is surely absurd to hold me "weak" or otherwise because I chose to persist in a study which I decided deliberately four or five years ago to make, next to my poetry, the most important pursuit of my life. If I had not made magic my constant

study I could not have written a single word of my Blake book, nor would *The Countess Kathleen* have ever come to exist.

He was not the only writer to be involved in the Golden Dawn. The others included Arthur Machen and Algernon Blackwood. (Intriguingly, Mrs. Oscar Wilde was also for a time a member, but probably had little influence on her husband in this respect.)

What kind of poetry did his Golden Dawn experience enable Yeats to write? I think that the most revealing approach is to examine the way it modified the basic Symbolist view of poetry Yeats shared with most of his literary contemporaries in fact, he shared a flat at one stage with Arthur Symons, the high prophet of Symbolism in England. The central tenet of Symbolism related to the poetic image. In contrast to the Victorians, especially perhaps Browning and Matthew Arnold whose attempts to justify their art made poetry argumentative, the poets of the 1890s were concerned to evoke images. Images were not necessarily related to public, shared experience but might be private and irrational. Indeed, it was characteristic of these images that they realized in large measure the Luciferic urge of the imagination and filled the whole consciousness of the artist; no room was left for argument or deliberation that was a part of their value to the writers weary of the old, endless dialectics. The image loomed large in the mind, and seemed able to absorb all reality into itself in a way that argument could never achieve.

Frank Kermode has shown that the Symbolist mode is a descendant of the Romantic image, the overwhelming inspiration.[5] Yet in its late nineteenth-century form, it represents a retreat from the full Romantic aspiration to give meaning to the whole range of human life and activity. It has become withdrawn, too purely Luciferic. Analogies between the Symbolist reverie and the quiescent mind of the Eastern mysticism that was flooding into Europe were recognized at the time. Mallarmé had already codified the relations between poetic and mystical evocation. At the same time, the benumbing of the deliberative faculties led to a moral instability, and to strange bifurcations, even to Jekyll-and-Hyde splittings of the personality. Yeats himself was to remark, "Muses resemble women who creep out at night and give themselves to unknown sailors and return to talk of Chinese porcelain": but, he added, in view of his own greater acceptance of reality, "the Muses sometimes form in those low haunts their most lasting attachments."

In his poetry of the 1890s, Yeats' images are spiritual presences, sometimes evoked by Golden Dawn meditations. Such presences include the ubiquitous Rose of Rosicrucian symbolism, which transmutes the agony of the cross into mystic beauty. As the proud, sad Rose it embraces Yeats' loneliness and his dreams of Celtic mythology, the noble purity of the old heroes. His inner training gives him the strength, however, not to yield to outright possession by the image. "To the Rose upon the Rood of Time" comes from his collection called *The Rose* (1893):

> Red Rose, proud Rose, sad Rose of all my days!
> Come near me, while I sing the ancient ways:
> Cuchulain battling with the bitter tide;
> The Druid, grey, wood-nurtured, quiet-eyed,
> Who cast round Fergus dreams, and ruin untold;
> And thine own sadness, whereof stars, grown old
> In dancing silver-sandalled on the sea,
> Sing in their high and lonely melody.
> Come near, that no more blinded by man's fate,
> I find under the boughs of love and hate,
> In all poor foolish things that live a day,
> Eternal beauty wandering on her way.
>
> Come near, come near, come near—

But now Yeats' consciousness asserts itself, remarkably overturning the movement of the poem's first part, insisting upon a space for itself and its earthly affiliations:

> Ah, leave me still
> A little space for the rose-breath to fill!
> Lest I no more hear common things that crave;
> The weak worm hiding down in its small cave,
> The field-mouse running by me in the grass,
> And heavy mortal hopes that toil and pass;
> But seek alone to hear the strange things said
> By God to the bright hearts of those long dead,
> And learn to chaunt a tongue men do not know,
> Come near; I would, before my time to go,
> Sing of old Eire and the ancient ways:
> Red Rose, proud Rose, sad rose of all my days.

In such poetry the Luciferic absorption is resisted, nirvana is postponed to make room for sympathy with the sorrows of the race according to the Rosicrucian ideal. The "poetry of earth" establishes a precarious hold on his imagination, but attains to a unique beauty under the growing Yeatsian sky, paving the way for the achievements of his later style.

The technique was extended to mastery in *The Wind Among the Reeds* (1899). Once again the poet is a magus, summoning some spirits and dispelling others. The motivic treatment Yeats adopts, where each poem creates a momentary personality and voice, with generalized titles such as "He Remembers Forgotten Beauty," or "He Thinks of his Past Greatness when a Part of the Constellations of Heaven," successfully diffuses any sense of Yeats' own presence, and looks forward to his symbolic presences: the wandering Aengus; the unappeasable Host; the white deer with no horns; the boar without bristles. Some poems, it is true, like "The Song of the Wandering Aengus," deal with the state of possession. But as Harold Bloom points out, the strength of the volume lies still in Yeats' "subtle, never quite spoken resistance to the 'sweet everlasting Voices' that have appropriated all of human passion, and yet left a man suffering in and from time."[6] A conscious space is created in the world of dream; but whereas most critics have assumed that this happens despite Yeats' occult training, it is actually a sign that the training was beginning to take effect.

I have described Symbolism as a retreat from the full claims of Romanticism, exemplified in Blake and Shelley, that Imagination is an apocalyptic power capable of "consuming" and remaking mundane reality. The Luciferic withdrawal was explored to the full by artists and poets of the late nineteenth century, those "dreamers of decadence" followers of Des Esseintes, the character created by Huysmans, who fashioned his own totally artificial world. Like the representatives of the culture around him, Yeats overcame the temptation to give in to the dream, and the victory is a direct outcome of his Rosicrucian inner training. Rudolf Steiner has described it as the mission of Rosicrucianism to be able to enter the Luciferic realm (from which art must draw) without suffering the loss of consciousness and moral purpose seen in most of Yeats' post-Romantic contemporaries.

Yet another struggle opens up before Yeats' inner gaze almost at once. Like Oisin in his own narrative poem, when he touches the earth on his return from the land of spirits, he is struck with infirmity and premature "old age." Consciousness is sustained, linking the spiritual with the earthly world, but as yet lacks power. It is not until he wrote "The Secret Rose," after nearly a decade of meditation on the Rosicrucian symbols, that he shows an imagination capable of bestowing not only awareness, but power. This further "invocation" is distinguished by the new confidence of its assertion, and the way Yeats no longer calls to the ancient heroes but numbers himself prophetically among their ranks:

> Far-off, most secret, and inviolate Rose,
> Enfold me in my hour of hours; where those
> Who sought thee in the Holy Sepulchre,
> Or in the wine-vat, dwell beyond the stir
> And tumult of defeated dreams; and deep
> Among pale eyelids, heavy with the sleep
> Men have named beauty. Thy great leaves enfold
> The ancient beards, the helms of ruby and gold
> Of the crowned Magi; and the King whose eyes
> Saw the Pierced Hands and Rood of elder rise
> In Druid vapour and make the torches dim;
> Till vain frenzy awoke and he died; and him
> Who met Fand walking among flaming dew
> By a grey shore where the wind never blew,
> And lost the world and Emer for a kiss;
> And him who drove the gods out of their liss,
> And till a hundred morns had flowered red
> Feasted, and wept the barrows of his dead;
> And the proud dreaming king who flung the crown
> And sorrow away, and calling bard and clown
> Dwelt among wing-stained wanderers in deep woods;
> And him who sold tillage, and house, and goods,
> And sought through lands and islands numberless years,
> Until he found, with laughter and with tears,
> A woman of so shining loveliness
> That men threshed corn at midnight by a tress,
> A little stolen tress. I, too, await
> The hour of thy great wind of love and hate.
> When shall the stars be blown about the sky,
> Like the sparks blown out of a smithy, and die?

> Surely thine hour has come, thy great wind blows,
> Far-off, most secret, and inviolate Rose?

The mythological fragments do not distract from the underlying movement and unity of the poem. Like Blake's, in his mythological lyrics, they evoke what seem overwhelmingly significant events, and prompt few questions. But if the largeness of scope recalls Blake, the allusions of the last lines make it clear that it is the prophetic mantle of Shelley which Yeats adopts.

Shelley's *Ode to the West Wind* calls upon the inspiring power to unite itself with the poet's conscious self ("Be thou me, impetuous one!"). This is not mystical union—the loss of self in the presence of the infinite— but the discovery of a power able to sustain the self in the encounter with otherness, which for Shelley, too, is an apocalyptic struggle. Yeats likewise identifies "my hour of hours" with "thine hour," the hour of the apocalyptic blast. The final question, and return to the words of the opening line, leaves the issue open; but the "Surely" signals the poet's sense of the inevitability of the struggle and its necessity for the future of his imaginative development. Henceforward he will fight his wars of the spirit against both dream and against "deformity," as he expressed the essence of ahrimanic distortion. Like Shelley, he noted the insidious pressure of the alien world upon the soul, compelling it to adopt shapes and colours inimical to its inner life. His poetic apocalypse was to point to the moment of the "brightening glance," when body and soul do not bruise each other in the quest of power, but are contained in the equilibrium that is at once wisdom and desire.

That moment seemed near around 1900, to many besides Yeats who characterized the time as "the trembling of the veil." By then, however, disaster was already brewing for the Hermetic Order of the Golden Dawn, and Yeats was called upon to act indeed though hardly as he had expected.

MacGregor Mathers had long been the most prominent "magician" in the Order, a position not contested by Westcott, the other founding member. (Dr. Woodman was by this time deceased.) Mathers was by now resident in Paris, continuing his activities and propagating Golden Dawn techniques. He organized a "Rite" of Isis, which was performed with great taste and refinement before a Paris theatre audience. He tried, with less success, to interest Henri Bergson, his brother-in-law, in magic. "I have shown him everything that magic can do," he later declared of the philosopher, "and it has had no effect on him." But he had other triumphs: in fact the Order was growing too large for him to keep under the control of his idiosyncratic personality. Too many questions were starting to be asked, too many demands made on him. Above all, his link with the higher Rosicrucian sources was being doubted. A committee of the adepts in London, including Yeats, was examining the Cypher manuscript, and some members were asking for a return to its contents alone—a kind of magic fundamentalism. Yeats himself had turned against Mathers before the crisis came to a head. In 1896 he had gone to Paris to plan with the magus a Celtic Mystery cult; they had proposed to create "an Irish Eleusis or Samothrace." The real fruit of this initiative was to be the Abbey Theater, beginning as a kind of Irish mystical and dramatic movement that was turned into reality with the financial support of another Golden Dawn adept, Annie Horniman (daughter of the tea magnate). It was to become one of the chief organs of the Irish movement in literature, and a source of inspiration to a generation of dramatists. By 1899, the original impulse had collapsed, however, and Yeats was disillusioned with Mathers. He subsequently rewrote the positive draft account of his *Autobiographies* dealing with him, emphasizing his eccentricities. This type of retrospective sitting in judgment is perhaps Yeats' least attractive side.

In 1900 came the final split. Mathers was discredited in the eyes of his London adepts because he had been forced to reveal the unreliability of the official version of the Golden Dawn's foundation. Unwisely, he attempted to right the boat by insisting on his own authority over the Order and sent—of all people—Aleister Crowley to take possession of the Temple's London premises, be it by persuasion, magic or force. Florence Farr took what seemed the best way of resisting all three and called a constable.

After this and other legal wrangles of 1900-1901, many retired from active magical service. And if the others who remained were able to move forward and recreate the Order, under the new name of the Stella Matutina (Morning Star), it was in no small measure owing to the unexpected and effective control asserted by Yeats, who now found himself being addressed by the revered title "Imperator" of the

Isis-Urania Temple, the Order's chief centre in London. Yeats seemed just to have found his true path, and his ability to work out of "dream" into the real world was not put to the test. After the break with Mathers, the whole question of the Order's foundation and authority was plunged into total darkness. If there was a way forward, the adepts had to establish it for themselves.

Then occurred a still harsher blow than the break with Mathers. In February 1903 Yeats received an unexpected letter from Paris to say that Maud Gonne had just married Major John MacBride. She had left him now not even the hopeless image of her purity, her oneness with the abstract cause of Ireland. Suddenly the revolutionaries he had idealistically supported looked like blind ruffians, without even the courage of the convictions he had been waiting for them to fulfill. He turned away from the nationalism with which she had been associated so long. He still could not repudiate the image in his soul of Maud Gonne. He wrote, however, with a new harshness of tone about her and the Irish situation, as in "No Second Troy":

> Why should I blame her that she filled my days
> With misery, or that she would of late
> Have taught to ignorant men most violent ways,
> Or hurled the little streets upon the great,
> Had they but courage equal to desire?
> What could have made her peaceful with a mind
> That nobleness made simple as a fire,
> With beauty like a tightened bow, a kind
> That is not natural in an age like this,
> Being high and solitary and most stern?
> Why, what could she have done, being what she is?
> Was there another Troy for her to burn?

Such is the style he evolved in the first decade of this century, more hard-bitten, and closer to speech rhythms than the evocations of *The Wind Among the Reeds*.

Without the glamour of his love for Maud Gonne, his fellow countrymen's aspirations looked philistine and prosaic enough. Let the language spoken to them be in their own vein! Other young poets and dramatists had already moved in the same, more colloquial direction. Yeats' verse of this period, in *The Green Helmet and Other Poems* (1910)

Maud Gonne

and *Responsibilities* (1914), is on the whole not his best. It has been praised for its modernity more than perhaps it deserves. But it did reflect his deep disillusion with the "blind, bitter land" in which he found himself, where he had always lived in spirit even when his magical and literary work kept him in London. Under the pressure of inner and outer developments, a whole phase of Yeats' life seemed to be coming to an end amid "the stir and tumult of defeated dreams." He needed all the inner strength his occult training had given him for his life and poetry over the next fourteen years. He had to rebuild the Hermetic Order as the Stella Matutina, and rebuild his own personality and capacity for love after the ravages of his passion for Maud Gonne.

PART II

It is often the case that a stray comment, or occasional remark, gives away more of the trend of our thoughts than does a carefully weighed declaration. One such instance, concerning the changes in Yeats' habit of thought, is surely the opening section of *Per Amica Silentia Lunae*, written in 1917 and developing the ideas that had rooted in Yeats' world over the previous few years.

He is discussing the way thoughts and images are evoked through the encounter with other people—usually people far removed in outlook from oneself, when "oneself" happens to be a poet and a diligent enquirer into the occult and magical. In the essays of *Per Amica* he develops this notion of productive encounter into the theory of the Daimon or contrary self. As he describes the experience first, he assumes momentarily that the "others" are male. After all, he had been an inveterate talker since his intellectual clashes with his father, and debated with the Rhymers' Club, with magicians, spiritists and spirits. Women, on the other hand, had characteristically been remote objects of worship and desire, from his adolescent poetry to the ultimate frustration of Maud Gonne; they had not shared his interests, or been accessible to intellectual companionship. Yet in 1917 Yeats adds revealingly to his encounter with his male fellow diners: "and sometimes even after talking to women." The "even" tells its own story, but the change is palpable evidence of Yeats' new sense of female company and anyone remotely familiar with his life will know the cause of it. He had at last found a woman he could talk to as well as love, who shared his preoccupations and spiritual needs. He had first met her in 1911, got to know her well a year or two later; and towards the end of 1917 he married her. He was fifty-two years old.

She was a young anthroposophist named Georgie Hyde-Lees, and Yeats' rather "giveaway" testimony to the effect of female conversation on his later thought returns us to the crisis of his life and occult development with a new perspective. We have seen how Yeats and his fellow adepts needed to find a "Rosicrucian" way forward from the impasse of the old Golden Dawn, and how Yeats himself rose to the leadership of one main group of *adepti*. He had found himself at the foot of a ladder, and the sense of clarity and power which came into his verse around the turn of the century proved the imaginative validity of his magical progress. The ensuing years, however, were even more demanding than the years of difficult exploration. A part of his success was undoubtedly the result of his contact with Rudolf Steiner—not least through the personal influence of Miss Hyde-Lees, or Mrs. "George" Yeats as she was generally known.

Already in the early 1900s a certain Dr. R. W. Felkin was becoming prominent among the adepts of the Stella Matutina. He was an intelligent man, with medical degrees from Edinburgh and Marburg and experience in Africa as a medical missionary, and he commanded respect among the stranded College of Adepts. He has been much criticized for his efforts to renew the Rosicrucian connection of the Golden Dawn; yet that was, after all, the basis of the Order, its whole claim to be more than a band of bold occult experimentalists. Dr. Felkin's sources pointed to Germany, and focused in particular on Dr. Rudolf Steiner.[1] Yeats was among those who supported him in his efforts to engineer an anthroposophical connection for the Order. The reasons are clear enough. Steiner had emphasized the Rosicrucian character of anthroposophy in many lecture cycles, and was from 1906 to 1914 the head of an esoteric "Memphis and Misraim" lodge in which he performed a Rosicrucian ritual. Steiner's rite was fundamentally different from those performed in similar lodges, but he had acquired a legitimate charter from Theodor Reuss. On a visit to Germany in 1910, and again in 1912, Felkin witnessed Steiner's ceremonies and entered into deep discussions with him about the future of the Stella Matutina. Steiner declined to take over the leadership of the Order, for reasons he makes clear in his autobiography. He gave no "grades" such as played a great part in Masonry, but agreed to advise Felkin and others on esoteric matters. He gave Felkin information, and spiritual exercises which could be used in the Stella Matutina to form the basis of rituals. It was on this foundation that Felkin devised the rite for the higher levels of the Order, the so-called *Adeptus Major* ritual. Yeats underwent his higher initiation in October 1914. A still higher rite, again based on the "continental processes," or forms given by Steiner, was ready in 1915. Yeats' experience of it was profound, and I have shown elsewhere that it formed the basis of his greatest poem, "Byzantium."[2]

It seemed that there need now be no barriers between the Anthroposophical Society and the Stella Matutina, at least in principle.

Various members of the Anthroposophical Society joined the Order, notably Harry Collison who supervised the whole connection. Georgie Hyde-Lees, already a committed anthroposophist, was initiated into the Golden Dawn in 1914. Over the next few years links were stepped up: in 1916 three new temples were opened in London, one specifically for members of the Anthroposophical Society. Evidently it was being found that the differing backgrounds of the two movements could "cause confusion," as Felkin tactfully put it. Meanwhile, for various reasons, Steiner had discontinued his own "Memphis and Misraim" lodge, though he continued to give esoteric teaching in other forms.

Yeats must have found much of Steiner's teaching immediately intelligible, and confirmation of his own Rosicrucian inner path. Steiner's teaching about the struggle of the spiritual self against the opposing forces of Lucifer and Ahriman came to meet his own discovery of the twin dangers of "dream" and "deformity"; much of the knowledge about the world after death was known to Yeats from earlier teachings and his own studies of the evidence of survival. But it is at the period of his growing love for the future Mrs. Yeats that many strikingly anthroposophical ideas begin to figure in the texture of his thought. Many of the concepts that appear in his extraordinary book *A Vision*, on which he worked from about 1917, are reminiscent of Steiner: the law of polarity, for instance, and the historical cycles or "gyres" in which the soul oscillates from incarnation to incarnation recall Steiner's teaching on the cultural epochs and echo their dating and sequence. It seems that Yeats tried to bring together evidence from different sources. He would spend considerable time and effort interrogating mediums (a very unanthroposophical approach) and then go to Georgie Hyde-Lees in the hope of confirming through her anthroposophical knowledge what they had said.[3]

At the same time, she also introduced him to ideas which became the themes for his later investigations. She almost certainly introduced him to the karma exercise given by Steiner in the 1912 course on *Reincarnation and Karma*. Steiner gave as one approach to finding one's previous incarnation an intensive imaginative effort, to be repeated many times, to "form a living conception of the man who has willed everything that we have not willed" (Lecture 2). Indeed, says Steiner, we must evoke the picture of the man who has willed the happenings and aspects of our lives which our conscious selves least want. This became that quest for the "Daimon" or contrary:

> of all imaginable things
> The most unlike, being my anti-self.

Much to Yeats' astonishment, the meditation came to quite concrete fruition. He met the imagination of Leo Africanus, the Renaissance Arab geographer, of whom he had never consciously heard. Leo was surprised and somewhat offended that Yeats did not know him. Unlike the sanguine and heavenward gazing visionary poet, Leo had spent his life plodding over and measuring the face of the earth.[4]

The case of Leo, who conversed with Yeats in trance and through mediums, is a good instance of the way that Steiner's influence on the poet was not so much a direct, intellectual one as a stimulus and a guide through the results of occult research. Most spectacularly, the "shared dream" or clairvoyant happenings at the basis of *A Vision*, while showing Steiner's growing importance in the background of his thought, takes his influence once more into the sphere of the poet's own imaginative and occult world. The principles it expounds were dictated by "spirits" through Mrs. Yeats. It has such deep similarity to Steiner's thought in his lectures on *Human and Cosmic Thought* that there is little doubt Mrs. Yeats' Daimon was reproducing unconsciously what she had imbibed from Anthroposophy. Yet far from being a mere copy of Steiner's dynamic or cosmic system of thought, what emerged from Yeats in response to the teachings was a complete transposition, so to speak, of Steiner's sun-and consciousness-centered imagery into terms of a moony half-light, to suit the needs of Yeats' still dreamier soul and his mystic Muse.

The experiences that lie behind *A Vision* were certainly shaped and crystallized into form by concepts learnt from Steiner. But the strange psychic experiences Yeats underwent also adapted the conscious frame-work to their own demands, and to the natures of those who shared them. If they could not retain the clairvoyant sun-clarity of Steiner's mind, however, neither did the images "take possession" of their souls. The "spirits" declared engagingly: "We come to give you metaphors for poetry," and required much hard work from Yeats to fill out the bare suggestions they dictated. Moreover, the communication was subject to detracting forces, against which Yeats' consciousness had perpetually to be vigilant. All in all, with *A Vision* the poet came further into the light of conscious spiritual vision than he had done before—though in comparison with Steiner's exact clairvoyant consciousness the book remains idiosyncratic and even rather quirky.

The real importance of *A Vision* lies not in what it achieves, but in the poems Yeats wrote in connection with its imagery and symbols. Its clarity combines with the deeper poetic insights Yeats was able to formulate. Above all, it helped in the meditations, continued over many years, which led to the great initiation poem of "Byzantium." Grounded in Yeats' experience of the Golden Dawn forms furnished by Steiner, it grew over many years to include much of the poet's essential wisdom and to express the inmost quality of his consciousness. Byzantine civilization was one of the moments "pricked" upon the gyres of history, a phase of fulfillment before the breakdown of forms once more and the emergence of a new epoch, in the system of *A Vision*. Afterwards comes our own self-conscious civilization. "Byzantium" points therefore to the greatness of what has been lost, and to what must be regained in a new way. What was once given to humanity in the sense of wholeness of being and cosmic significance must henceforth be won by inner effort and conscious struggle. Our own phase of civilization, Yeats foresaw, would be marked by terrible struggles in every sphere of life, especially around the time of crisis he describes as the incarnation of the Antichrist, the Ahrimanic "rough beast" described in "The Second Coming." Kathleen Raine asserts that Yeats believed that time would be the end of the twentieth century.

Appropriately for an initiation poem, "Byzantium" is dominated by a tremendous effort of consciousness, and by a struggle with the elemental powers of the depths which threaten to overwhelm mere human consciousness. But it begins in the calmness of meditation. The poet imagines himself standing in Byzantium in the fading light of evening:

> The unpurged images of day recede;
> The Emperor's drunken soldiery are abed;
> Night resonance recedes, night-walkers' song
> After great cathedral gong;
> A starlit or a moonlit dome disdains
> All that man is,
> All mere complexities,
> The fury and the mire of human veins.

The poet's consciousness does not fade with the dying light. The stillness of the poetry conceals the effort of consciousness to sustain itself as the images of sense fall away. Awareness is increased rather than lessened, and reaches out into the cosmic spaces. The unpurged images (ordinary perception) will gradually be transformed in the poem into the living, self-renewing images which point to a higher, supersensible reality:

> Those images that yet
> Fresh images beget.

In between, however, the poet-initiate must fight to master the forces of his own nature and those of the worlds into which he is entering.

On one level it is a struggle with the powers of bodily nature. From these the spirit must not so much break free, as learn to master: to "ride" as Blake had shown the spirit-child riding the serpent of man's lower nature. The struggle is against flesh and blood ("the fury and the mire of human veins"), which grows in the poet's imagination into the torrent of the dark waters, the "flood" which must be "broken" by the work of the artist, creative of beauty from the surging chaos. This flood-imagery appears elsewhere in Yeats' verse, for example, in *The Delphic Oracle upon Plotinus*:

> Behold that great Plotinus swim
> Buffed by such seas;
> Bland Rhadamanthus beckons him,
> But the Golden Race looks dim,
> Salt blood blocks his eyes.
> Scattered on the level grass
> Or winding through the grove
> Plato there and Minos pass,
> There stately Pythagoras
> And all the choir of Love.

The buffeting sea again stands for physical life, to be battled through by the heavenly spirit of the ancient mystic and philosopher. It derives in fact from an authentic oracle of Apollo at Delphi, in which the god spoke in precisely these terms after the death of Plotinus. But how has Yeats come to connect this divine obituary and its symbolism with his initiation poem? It appears that he is again developing ideas from Rudolf Steiner, which helps us understand the inner working of his

Byzantium poem. In particular, it helps us understand that brilliant image of the dolphin leap of the spirit in the last stanza:

> Astraddle on the dolphin's mire and blood
> Spirit after spirit!

At one time Steiner was clearly much concerned with the myth of Apollo at Delphi, for he discussed the meaning of the legends in his course *Christ and the Spiritual World* and in other cycles of the period (1913-1914, i.e., the very time his work, circulated in ad hoc translations, was having most effect on Mr. and Mrs. Yeats). The materials have been collected by Karl König in a book recently published in English. The myths are about the slaying of the dragon Python by Apollo, and also with the god's epiphanies in the form of a dolphin, that creature of the deeps which is nevertheless a friend to man. König summarizes Steiner on the ancient myths as follows:

> The myths speak of two different dragons dwelling at the foot of Mount Parnassus: one a male named Python, the other female, named Delphyne. She was regarded as the greatest enemy of Apollo. In order to overcome this dragon, Apollo had to transform himself into it. This was the power that ruled over forces of nature which preside over blind processes of self-reproduction and birth, in their continual repetitions. (For *delphos* is the womb). From this "dolphin" form Apollo rises free, like a star, becoming its master. Thus through the Pythoness—

the prophetess at the Delphic oracle—

> the otherwise unbridled reproductive powers of the feminine nature, overcome by the sun-god were able to speak. Thus the image of Apollo lives on in the consciousness of the Greeks and of later peoples as slayer of the dragon. Rudolf Steiner describes this. ... Apollo had to transform himself into "Delphyne." In this way he won the power to conquer the Python.[5]

The struggles mythically enacted by Apollo, according to Steiner's interpretation, correspond exactly to those of Yeats' initiation and his Byzantium poem. Like Yeats, Steiner does not believe that the way to overcome the dragons, the forces of natural birth and death, is to abandon the natural world. Rather, the natural and spiritual must be fused into a higher vision comprehending both.

Whilst registering its darker side, Steiner represents the myth as meaning that Apollo had to become Delphyne, to unite himself with the forces of chaos to wring from it order and beauty. And thus Yeats:

> Astraddle on the dolphin's mire and blood
> Spirit after spirit! The smithies break the flood,
> The golden smithies of the Emperor!
> Marbles of the dancing floor
> Break bitter furies of complexity,
> Those images that yet
> Fresh images beget,
> That dolphin-torn, that gong-tormented sea.

The world of ordinary perception disintegrates like the broken fragments of mosaic. Human beings must acknowledge the dark forces of their own depths. But we see human consciousness able to break the flood, and flash upward into awareness of its celestial origin, rising free like a star as the animal falls away.

Yeats' relation to Rudolf Steiner's thought has been a strangely neglected subject. Yet he was drawn to it by the whole direction of his life's work, and there is much valuable light to be shed on Yeats' thought and art from the consideration of Steiner's influence. It remains an area where much research is still needed, which will no doubt illuminate the deeper significance of one of the greatest poetic imaginations of modern times.

* * *

This article includes material also appearing in the journal *Theosophical History,* by kind permission of the editor.

Notes—Part I

1. I have written at greater length of the links between Rudolf Steiner and Yeats in my forthcoming book *The Truth of Imagination: Introduction to Visionary Poetry* (New York: Macmillan/St. Martin's Press). Generally for Yeats' life, ideas and poetry, see the brilliant biography by Richard Ellmann, *Yeats: The Ms*(New York: Norton, 1979). New editions of Yeats' works are appearing, notably *The Poems,* ed. Richard Finneran (London, 1984); and editions are promised of the *Autobiographies,* the Plays and *A Vision,* as well as a comprehensive collection of the letters.

2. Yeats himself, of course, was subsequently a major influence and organizing power in the Irish Movement, often called "the Celtic Twilight," after Yeats' book of that title.

3. Israel Regardie, *My Rosicrucian Adventure* (St. Paul, MN: Llewellyn, 1971), 69. Yeats' role in the Golden Dawn has been exhaustively documented by G. Mills Harper, *Yeats' Golden Dawn* (New York: Barnes & Noble, 1974), but it is well worth looking at Ellic Howe, *Magicians of the Golden Dawn* (London: Routledge & Kegan Paul, 1972: a more recent paperback edition, 1985) and Francis King, *Ritual Magic in England* (London: Spearman, 1970). And see Kathleen Raine, *Yeats the Initiate* (London: G. Allen and Unwin, 1986).

4. Ellman, *Yeats: The Man and the Masks*, 96.

5. See Frank Kermode, *Romantic Image* (London: Routledge, 1971): a brilliant little book with much on Yeats.

6. Harold Bloom, *Yeats* (New York: Oxford University Press, 1970), 125.

Notes—Part II

1. See Ellic Howe, *Magicians of the Golden Dawn*, 240ff, 255ff. Howe admits that Felkin was highly regarded by his fellow initiates. Regardie, *My Rosicrucian Adventure*, 142, points out that the role of Felkin and Steiner in Golden Dawn affairs was first uncovered by Virginia Moore, and remarks that the connection with Steiner "was a rather ironic impasse for the Golden Dawn initiates to be brought to." This is hardly justified, since long before, a positive attitude toward Steiner was present high up among the "founding fathers": see, for instance, Wynn Westcott's review of Steiner's teaching for a Masonic leadership, now republished in R.A. Gilbert *The Magical Mason* edited by R. A. Gilbert (Wellingborough, Northants: Aquarian Press, 1983). Howe is hostile to Felkin too, seemingly because he does not fit with Howe's own cherished thesis, namely, that everything of any value in the Golden Dawn derived from MacGregor Mathers. Hence the idea of the Golden Dawn after and without Mathers was for him a nonsense. However, in the above sketch I have endeavored to adopt a different perspective—one that fits the evidence about Felkin better.

2. The origins of the poem are discussed by Ellmann, *Yeats: The Man and the Masks*, 225, but without reference to the sources of the Golden Dawn initiation. I have quoted materials from Steiner analogues to Yeats' sketch and to the complete poem in my *The Truth of Imagination*. The "Memphis and Misraim" ritual which Rudolf Steiner performed, and, indeed, this whole phase of his work is now a good deal less mysterious than it was since

the publication of *Zur Geschichte und aus den Inhalten der ersten Abteilung der Esoterischen Schuler* (GA 264) (1984) and *Zur Geschichte und aus den Inhalten der erkenntniskultischen Abteilung der Esoterischen Schule* (GA 265) (Dornach 1987). It is doubtful whether one can, at any stage, call Rudolf Steiner a Freemason in the accepted sense of the term. Cf the remarks of Manfred Schmidt-Brabant, *Die Drei* (1988),4.

3. Ellmann, *Yeats*, 219. Ellmann's reference to Miss Hyde-Lees as belonging in 1914 to the "Rudolf Steiner Theosophists" is of course nominally inaccurate. From February 1913, one must speak of Steiner's followers as constituting the independent Anthroposophical Society.

4. See Ellmann, 194ff, and for more detail, my *The Truth of Imagination*. I also discuss there the origins of some of the elements of the teaching in *A Vision*. Full transcripts (insofar as they are available) of the material have now been published, ed. G. Mills Harper (London, 1987). Richard Ellmann told me, however, that he thought Mrs. Yeats in later years destroyed some papers relating to the communications.

5. Karl König, *Seals, Dolphins, Salmon and Eels* (Edinburgh: Floris, 1984), 86-87.

From Et La Lumiere Fut

Jacques Lusseyran

(Editor's Note) A few years ago, Oliver Sachs published an essay in The New Yorker *entitled "The Mind's Eye: What the Blind See," an exploration of the extraordinary powers of perception that the blind sometimes develop. One of the remarkable stories Sachs weaves into the piece is that of the French philosopher Jacques Lusseyran. Born in Paris in 1924, Lusseyran was blinded in an accident when he was eight years old. At 16, after the German occupation of France, he organized and led an underground resistance movement. He was betrayed, arrested by the Gestapo, and deported to Buchenwald where he remained until its liberation. He writes movingly about all this in his autobiography* And There Was Light *and in essays collected under the title* Against the Pollution of the I.[1] *Most remarkable of all is his account of how the loss of his eyesight brought a miraculous gain in other powers, including a new kind of sight, a seeing without eyes. Sachs' essay is worth quoting:*

> *Lusseyran inveighs against the "despotism," the "idol worship," of sight, and sees the "task" of blindness as reminding us of our other, deeper modes of perception and their mutuality. "A blind person has a better sense of feeling, of taste, of touch," he writes, and speaks of these as "the gifts of the blind." And all of these, Lusseyran feels, blend into a single, fundamental sense, a deep attentiveness, a slow, almost prehensile attention, a sensuous, intimate being at one with the world which sight, with its quick, flicking, facile quality, continually distracts us from.[2]*

What follows is an excerpt from Lusseyran's Et La Lumiere Fut[3] *which describes a two-week visit, at the age of 13, to Dornach, Switzerland. The passage was omitted from the British and American editions.*

. ... In 1937, at the age of thirteen, I went on a journey that holds a peculiarly unique place in my life. My parents and I traveled to

Dornach, a Swiss village not far from Basel. There, at the top of a hill, rose a singular building: the Goetheanum. Rudolf Steiner had had it built, in order to have a place for the working and meeting together of all those who followed his teachings. He himself had spoken there. And he spoke; he did not prophesy. In a wonderfully simple, completely sober method of speaking, he showed that spiritual worlds do exist. Deliberately and without pathos he affirmed with quiet force that it is the spiritual worlds that determine our physical one. He explained what these spiritual worlds consist of, why we generally know nothing of them, and the reasons for our ignorance and its significance. But now the time had come, he said, to openly reveal these secrets, which had been withheld up to now by a small number of initiates.

By birth Rudolf Steiner was an Austrian and in the German language he held hundreds and hundreds of lectures in which he seemed never to invent but rather to describe spontaneously what was before his eyes at the very moment. Dornach, in its wreath of surrounding hills, still cherished the traces of his earthly path in a way that was profound yet not austere, respectful yet not idolizing.

My father had for many years been active and influential in the French section of the Anthroposophical Society. He devoted all his free time to a regular lecturing schedule. To me, too, he spoke a great deal about Steiner and his work. Gradually I began to understand more and more, and a quiet and unforced veneration filled my mind. The teachings of this astonishing man—at least, those that impressed me at the time— struck me with a feeling unknown until then: namely, a feeling of certainty, a feeling that the teachings were self-evident. The cycle of successive reincarnations, in particular, gave me complete tranquility. I can still experience it today. For in accord with this new insight, any indignation about earthly injustice and unmerited suffering is wiped away. The misfortune that meets us can only be measured by our own responsibility; our anxiety and despair are now revealed to be a result of our ignorance. We must pay for our past mistakes and answer for our present faults, but we shall be able to atone for them in a future life.

Even if our outward, visible history seems absurd and arbitrary, our inner destiny knows only equilibrium and compensation. To some extent we are masters of our own personal fate; we are no longer—as so many religions would teach—condemned to exist, to be born, to die. Instead we are guilty only when given over entirely to matter and forgetful of our essential Self. And thus eternity is no longer so inexplicably projected into the future but rather encompasses our life on all sides, this life of ours which is at once so trivial and so significant.

I used to listen to these teachings, one after the other, but without ever summoning in myself the will to accept them. I was not fostering a belief. I was merely willing to see what was shown to me. Life itself would decide my choice.

I spent two weeks in Dornach and paid careful attention to everything. One event, however, absorbed my interest more than anything else. I was allowed to attend a eurythmy performance. On an ordinary theatre stage in the Goetheanum, men and women were dancing, or rather, they seemed to dance. For eurythmy was not stylized choreography, but an art, a new art, just as complete and original an art as poetry or music. Steiner had created its foundations and established its first laws. It could be said that eurythmy reconciles word and motion; a particular movement of the body corresponds to each spoken sound, making poetry or prose visual, pictorial. There was, accordingly, a eurythmy alphabet based on the inner spiritual meaning of the sounds of speech, and a freely applied grammar to hold them together. Sometimes the eurythmists developed their art in connection with music, sometimes with a recited poem.

On that evening, poems by Goethe and also several by Steiner himself were recited. They touched me deeply, for without quite understanding them (they were spoken in German) I could guess their meaning without any effort. The speakers brought the words to life through gestures of the hand or the arm or with the whole body.

The German language immediately seemed to me of an extraordinary, musical beauty; most of all, it seemed imbued with a miraculous and unique flexibility. It never sounded finite, never closed or dead. It brought sounds into uninterrupted motion, rich in invention. It let them rise or sink in an uninterrupted flow, always following certain curves that were impossible to predict. Though often rough and sometimes heavy or, at least, ponderous, it struck the air with solemn drumbeats. But it was never satisfied with itself; it seemed always to be in search of and following its moving forms.

Its grace beguiled me. Yes, I say: its grace—certainly not that brilliant and proportioned grace of the French language, but more ardent, more willed. I heard how the vowels or the warm diphthongs, ü, ä, ö, following a slow, very determined rhythm, soften the piano-like tones of the st, pf, cht; how at other times they put their feet on the ground and emphasize their strength in the endings -g or -t: *Wirkung, aufgebaut*. German became for me the language of a musician-architect, to whom the speech sounds have given building-stones and an impulse of will, so that he can patiently erect his speech edifice.

Through all this I was filled with an enthusiasm which was to last for almost ten years without diminishing—and which today can still seize me at any opportunity. I simply had a passion for the German language. Soon there followed a passion for Germany as well, and for everything it conceals of menace and of treasure. I found myself confronted with a mystery. ...

Notes

1. *And There Was Light* (New York: Parabola Books, 1998) and *Against the Pollution of the I: Selected Writings of Jacques Lusseyran* (New York: Parabola Books, 1999).

2. Oliver Sachs, "The Mind's Eye: What the Blind See," *The New Yorker*, 28 July, 2003.

3. Jacques Lusseyran, *Et La Lumiere Fut* (Paris: Edition La Table Ronde, 1953).

Word Wisdom

Nathan Lyons

Romantic Religion: A Study of Barfield, Lewis, Williams, and Tolkien by R. J. Reilly (Athens: University of Georgia Press, 1971), 249 pages.

T his welcome and thoughtful book deserves a serious reading by all concerned with the crosscurrents of literature and religion in our times. It is particularly welcome for its inclusion of what is probably the first major study of Owen Barfield's work by a significant academician not traveling the anthroposophical path.

R. J. Reilly, Professor of English at the University of Detroit, has thoughtfully explored those men sometimes called the Oxford Christians: C. S. Lewis and Charles Williams (both Anglicans), J. R. R. Tolkien (a Roman Catholic), and Owen Barfield. Since Barfield is the least well-known (and, I believe, the figure Reilly finds most pertinent) the first main chapter, "Owen Barfield and Anthroposophical Romanticism," is devoted to him. Reilly notes that C. S. Lewis, one of the most respected of modern literary figures, placed Barfield with G. K. Chesterton and George MacDonald as the most important conscious influences on his work and mind; and Lewis' *Allegory of Love,* that superior exegesis of the medieval courtly tradition, is dedicated to Barfield, "the wisest and best of my unofficial teachers." Yet Barfield's own work has until now suffered that neglect caused by a "combination of a refusal to investigate with readiness to dismiss" that Barfield once noted has been Rudolf Steiner's fate.

It is interesting that though Reilly appears less enthusiastic about Steiner than Barfield, he has made an effort to "investigate" Steiner, with Barfield as his Virgil, for he properly recognizes the acknowledged indebtedness of the one to the other. Though for Reilly (as for C. S. Lewis) Steiner's work suffers from a "Germanic dullness," he presents and explicates a number of fundamental concepts with scholarly accuracy. It is, in fact, Reilly's very willingness to investigate that, for me, represents one of the most appealing events in recent scholarly achievement, supporting my own view that the indifference and coolness toward anthroposophic ideas has taken a long overdue turn. (Warner Berthoff, Professor of English at Harvard and a

Owen Barfield and C. S. Lewis on a Walking Tour

specialist in Melville and the Transcendentalists, wrote me recently that he was interested in some comments of mine on anthroposophy, "having just recently run into Owen Barfield's chapters on Rudolf Steiner. Not a bad commitment for an explorer of American Transcendentalism, among other topics, or for a conscientious teacher." Berthoff, like others in the American academic world, had simply not heard of Steiner before reading Barfield.) On a number of issues, Reilly thinks Barfield is clearer than Steiner; it is possible, one might add, that from the defined (and limited) perspective of most English professors in America, Barfield will inevitably be the figure who initiates an interest in anthroposophy.

Barfield's work, says Reilly, "may really be called anthroposophy philologically considered." At its root is a penetrating study of the evolution of human consciousness, a study of the "secrets hidden in language" that show the true non-Darwinian evolution of mankind. The Reformation's "insistence on the inwardness of all true grace," for instance, and the subsequent and "steady shifting inwards of the center of gravity in human consciousness" stands revealed in language and reveals a defined evolutionary process.

Reilly notes the essential study in Barfield's work, from his earliest book, *History in English Words* (1926) to his recent *Speaker's Meaning* (1967), and that Barfield repeatedly stresses the validity of the "creative imagination." Poetry involves the "bringing farther into consciousness of something which already exists as unconscious life"; and since God, for Barfield, is not wholly outside but immanent in man's unconscious, this creative imagination becomes not strictly an aesthetic process but a way in which man can participate in the divine process; "romanticism and religion," says Reilly, "are for him almost interchangeable terms, "and the study of poetry and the aesthetic process throughout history, philologically and epistemologically, thus becomes a study of the way in which man has discovered that God's nature and power are "within partial reach of the human will and imagination." In Barfield, notes Reilly, "man participates in God by means of the imagination—more and more consciously since the Incarnation." In our time, *romanticism comes of age*; "wisdom is no longer only *theosophia* but *anthroposophia*, not only the wisdom of God but also the wisdom of man"; and "God's progressive creation of the world, in fact, occurs through the human imagination."

These are telling perceptions, and it is good to think of them taking their place within the modern literary and theological dialogue, so often barren and materialistic. It establishes a qualitative relationship between man and God—indeed, between man and "meaning" and nature and the Cosmos.

Sanderson, in Barfield's *Worlds Apart* (1963), says that "Steiner is more like a natural phenomenon than an ordinary writer or lecturer"—a phrase, interestingly, that the American poet Jones Very used to describe Shakespeare (and to place him beyond the priggish carping of those nineteenth-century moralists who were concerned with the lack of moral judgment in the bard). Barfield, whom Reilly rightly calls an excellent example of Emerson's "Man thinking," has drawn substance and directions from the "natural phenomenon" and elaborated, with particular emphasis on philology, Steiner's ideas on the evolution of consciousness. This is the healthy use of anthroposophy Steiner envisioned—not ever a slavish *bondage* to his ideas, but their creative development. If R. J. Reilly has perhaps failed to appreciate the full dimensions of the source, he has brilliantly illumined one of its fairest fruits. *Romantic Religion* is an extremely important book, which, one hopes, will herald a new era in which the ideas of Rudolf Steiner will truly take their place in the broad international dialogue of serious men seeking paths through the chaos and paths into the future.

A Voice of Anthroposophy

George O'Neil

Unancestral Voice by Owen Barfield (Middletown, CT: Wesleyan University Press, 1965).

There is a new book out to enjoy and to pass on to friends. A fascinating yarn, ruggedly honest, and as tough going in spots as any lawyer, physicist, theologian, or better-world liberal would want. Owen Barfield brings an extraordinary assortment of gifts: a steel-trap legal mind, a poet's link with the spirit of speech, and an uncanny eye for people. And he is able to weave it together in a haunting story pattern. One can understand Wesleyan University Press being willing to risk the off-beat substance, the anthroposophy. More writers of this caliber and artistry, and what a different, what an other world it would be! For those, that is, who belong to the future, and search out the seed-points of things to come.

Barfield has done half a dozen volumes on language, history, and the evolution of consciousness as reflected in the human being's ways of using thought. *Worlds Apart*, the most recent, was a study of watertight mental compartments among professionals. A delightful weekend dialogue-war, one that can be read aloud for the sheer joy of the characterizations, the Babel of separate tongues in current disciplines. *Unancestral Voice* carries on. Burgeon, the lawyer-linguist host, again tells the story. The dialogue continues, but stepped up. The problem: the creative mind's relation to its own source of illumination. And isn't this the gist of Rudolf Steiner's contribution? Must not the productive person of today find an individual voice of ideas? Isn't this the survival question?

The topics and themes we must leave to the reader's adventure. But one point deserves mention. The composition of ideas treated is beautifully organic, living. The book grows. It roots in raw social facts, such as the swamp of sexuality seeping into culture, the delinquency of kids without tradition and authority during the time they need to respect it, and crime and the virulence of the pro and con among those who would meet it. After the facts, come the riddles of time and evolution and the actual meaning of history—changes in human beings from age to age. The book culminates then on the blossoming of the human spirit, the crisis today in science, in thinking. The outlook is dim or radiant depending on how we choose. And the choice—there's no question there—is prejudice or insight. Openness to new ideas. The result of such an unfolding development of thoughts is the aftereffect on the reader. Because of the viable form, they can live on and work. The book digests well.

As a storytelling device we are introduced to 16th century Maggidism. A little known biography of Joseph Karo is quoted. A lawyer-mystic in whom the voice of the angel spoke. Burgeon's source of intuitive ideas progressively grows objective, becomes a dialogue within the mind. He personifies it. In this way anthroposophy, the knowledge that the spirit of the human being generates to lead into the spirit of the world, can be introduced in novel form. And it has charm. The Meggid, as he names the entity, is lovable. And he or she (one is not sure which) is often provoked by Burgeon's thick-headedness. One thing this sort of device permits is to show in picture form the stages by which the intuitive process develops. First, in the quiet of the morning hours the Voice speaks. Speaks in pure thought, which must be translated into awkward earth words. After various courtings and encounters, it sinks deeper. During the history discourse on shipboard (taking off from Toynbee) Burgeon really "gets going." He is surprised at his own eloquence and learning, begins to realize he's been helped in the debate on theology and timelessness. A third phase comes in the crisis among the scientists in the lecture hall. Burgeon's young friend has been worked into a corner during his lecture on the crisis in micro-physics. Can inspiration work at a distance ... as a field-effect? It is a dramatic moment, especially for the future of science. So runs the illumination of the man Burgeon.

There will be difficulties for some. The language is pure English. The provenance of the substance is Steiner's German. Much seems strange at first until one remembers that for good translation the writer must return to the same sources from which the original stemmed: the idea. But this more or less is the theme of the book. Perhaps the science of things of the spirit will first flourish here on the wings of the Western world. The Meggid as angel of the Logos would care for that.

Another difficulty may be raised for others. That of acknowledgment of source. In *Worlds Apart*, Sanderson does acknowledge at length and sharply his Steinerian source, and wrestles with the question of how long an idea or perception must live in you before it becomes indigenous. Here Steiner goes unmentioned, although the Meggid on the final page reveals itself as the voice of *anthroposophia*. Does this separate the teachings from the name? But the writer stands by his lifework. A novel emerges from the man. What one has experienced in one's fibers is one's own. And the source stands written in broad script for all with the sense to see.

For members and friends the book has special value. The language of anthroposophy was re-formed every decade during Steiner's life. It was part of his genius to achieve this. Today too, to live and work, spirit must find new formulations. For study-circles and talk-sessions we've been provided with a fine challenge to learn how anthroposophy can sound in the 60's and 70's. And how it can be spoken to and be received by ears attuned to the patois of the day.

An Interview with Andrei Tarkovsky*

Translated and introduced by Marton Radkai

Over the years the anthroposophical movement has attracted a vast array of individuals ranging from farmers and factory workers and owners to politicians, lawyers, and artists. Filmmakers, by contrast, appear to have been absent from the ranks. Recently, the Russian film director Andrei Tarkovsky made it known that Steiner's writings were the inspiration for his next film, *The Sacrifice*.

Under the scrutiny of the camera, Andrei Tarkovsky's face seems carved from stone. Only the wiry moustache and deep-set inquisitive and sad eyes soften the sinews that frame his mouth. His jaws appear clenched together. History and inner struggles have chiseled him. He was born in the Soviet Union in 1932, too young to be a soldier but old enough to be conscious of the wrath of World War II. As a young man his interests ranged from geology and prospecting in Siberia to the study of music, painting, and Arabic. He finally settled in the field of cinema where he has remained for the past twenty-three years.

Tarkovsky scored his first major film success in 1967 with the screen adaptation of the life of the 15th-century iconographer Andrei Roublev. On the basis of that film, French critic and author Georges Sadoul placed Tarkovsky in the pantheon of Soviet filmmakers alongside Sergei Eisenstein and Pudhovkin. Since *Roublev*, Tarkovsky has established himself with *Solaris* (1972), *The Mirror* (1974), *The Stalker* (1980), and most recently *Nostalghia* (1983) for which he won Cannes' Golden Palm award. Like some of his filmmaking colleagues (Zefirelli and the late Visconti), Tarkovsky has also been active in theater and opera, directing

---

*This interview took place in 1985, the year before Tarkovsky died.

a Covent Garden production of Mussorgsky's *Boris Godunov* in November 1983.

Some have called his films depressing; others have commended them for their mysterious, dense, rich, and poetic qualities. There is no doubt however that Tarkovsky's films have consistently sidestepped the dictates of Socialist Realism, resulting in only cool support from Soviet administrators. Cold-shoulder treatment came to a head in Cannes where, after being urged to present *Nostalghia* by the minister of culture, Tarkovsky found that the Soviet jury member was none other than Bondarchuk, his archenemy! On July 11, 1984, at a news conference in Rome, he announced that he was not returning to Russia.

His defection was ironic. In an interview three months earlier, he had spoken of *Nostalghia* (nostalgia) as a "fatal illness" that strikes those who leave behind their homeland and sever their roots. This individual scenario he sees also in global terms:

> It is not normal that this planet is divided into two spheres of influence. It is abnormal because it is not the human being who created this earth. Man has no right over it. His only right is to live on earth and cultivate its spirituality. And not to divide our planet with barbed wire and to protect the division with nuclear weapons. That is inhuman.

Tarkovsky's preoccupation with the human condition in the broadest sense and his perception of established philosophies as providing little opportunity for changing or ameliorating the human condition led him in his search for a fresh path, whereby he came upon anthroposophy. The following is an interview of Andrei Tarkovsky by Nathan Federovsky.

Nathan Federovsky: Andrei Tarkovsky, what is it that fascinates you in the personality of Rudolf Steiner? How do you explain the fact that interest in the anthroposophical outlook is growing?

Andrei Tarkovsky: How can one explain the uncommon interest in Steiner? No one today can deny the fact that humankind has taken the wrong road. Everyone from the schoolchild to the head of state knows that we are stuck at an impasse, in a crisis. Also, it is no secret that human evolution has progressed asynchronously—by which I mean that the material and spiritual aspects of evolution have more often than not had little to do with one another and have reached different levels of influence. The material aspect has remained at the forefront in every respect—philosophical, technical, and cultural—whereas the spiritual aspect has been treated in a perfunctory manner or else completely ignored. Some even believe that man possesses no spiritual being at all! On the other hand, many others have come to the conclusion that it is erroneous to think that a human being's life is bound to his brief physical existence.

Steiner offers a worldview that explains everything, or at least *almost* everything, and gives appropriate space for human evolution in the spiritual realm. This outlook has attracted many followers in Germany, but not only in Germany; today there are anthroposophical schools in Sweden, France, the USA, Israel—everywhere, and that is not surprising. While in earlier times one could seriously adopt a materialistic position and explain the meaning of life and society on a material basis, today this is no longer possible. Today we need other perspectives; we must develop our spiritual lives and then ask the question, what is the meaning of existence? For when it is said that life evolves according to the rules of matter, it implies that life has no meaning. No one who has thought of it even a little can agree with the view that life in and of itself is without meaning.

For example, when someone tells me: "No, your life is not meaningless because you are sacrificing yourself so that future generations can live better," it is absurd and unacceptable, since it implies that those who physically sacrifice themselves have no right to live for a higher goal. To sacrifice oneself for someone else is wonderful, but it does not suffice. It is far more important to develop oneself spiritually than to become the fodder for future generations. ...

Of course, if one does not believe in the soul's immortality the question is irrelevant and it becomes pointless to speak in such categories. However, when this half-heartedness and materialism no longer satisfy, we may think further and grasp that the crisis of the modern world is rooted in the conflict between the spiritual and the material. Without harmony between these two, the meaning of life cannot be grasped. Steiner dedicated his whole life to the task of speaking about the meaning of human existence, of revealing what a spiritual person can achieve in this life, what he should strive for and what can offer him perspective and hope. To come back to the initial point: the flowering of anthroposophy shows the crisis of bourgeois values in the West, of affluence, of conformity, of perpetual consuming. ... Steiner not only criticizes those who conceive of life in materialistic terms but also opposes, as few have, the material wealth that Western democracy has spawned. I do not want to imply that Western democracy is bad; it's the best this planet has to offer, but it nevertheless does sometimes lead to tragic conflicts and places us in hopeless situations.

NF: We're approaching the problems you treat in your new film. Your camera will soon roll in Sweden. The title *The Sacrifice* has to do with some of the things we just spoke about.

AT: The film I want to make now centers on the fact that the modern human being can make no decisions in life. He casts his vote and chooses for himself the people who will be in government, who then act primarily in the interests of their party or social stratum. In general then—this applies to intellectuals as well—we surrender control over our own lives to professional politicians who have usurped the right to care for the well-being of the masses. Even if we make some claims to individualism, the life of modern human beings depends entirely on these others. Not to speak of the ever-worsening East-West conflict, in which no ordinary person has any influence. In the film I tell of a person who attempts to participate in life, to influence the destiny of those close to him, even the destiny of a nation; this person wants to be involved in life and alter its course. This is only possible if he understands that no one can do anything for him as long as he does not do something himself.

That is what my film is about; if we do not want to live as parasites on the body of society, nourished by the fruits of democracy, if we do not want to become conformists and consumer-idiots, we will have to renounce many things—and we must begin with ourselves. We are always quick to place blame on others—society, our friends ... but not ourselves. On the contrary, we especially enjoy lecturing and advising others on their behavior; we want to be prophets but have no right to it because we pay the least attention to ourselves and fail to follow our own advice. ... What is a good person today? Only when one is ready to sacrifice oneself can one claim to influence the overall life processes; there is no other way. Otherwise the massive lead ball of events will gather such momentum and speed that it will be impossible to stop. ... As a rule the price we will have to pay is our material well-being.

At the very least one should live what one preaches so that principles are not just babble and demagogy, but realities. This is Tolstoy's famous conflict. All of his life, Tolstoy suffered because he was a wealthy landowner who earned money from his books. It was the terrible conflict between him and his wife, Sofia Andreyewna. Today something similar is taking place. We are all decent people keeping up good appearances. We heap condemnation and praise on others, and we each forget ourselves. That is why our society lacks healthy perspectives. They can only be found when we understand that everything depends on each one of us in spite of the fact that each of us is one among billions. That's what the film is about, even though the plot is not linked word for word to this theme. Whoever hears or reads this interview might wonder about the subject matter.

NF: The title of the film, The *Sacrifice*, suggests that the hero carries out a specific deed, although a life in and of itself can be a sacrifice if one has renounced something.

AT: In the film it is a deed. The sacrifice is in fact always a deed. Even if you settle down somewhere in the lotus position, close your eyes and starve, that is a deed although one could say that you are distancing yourself from life. On the other hand, I do not believe in the noble convictions of the politician who babbles on about hunger in Ethiopia and then goes off to a champagne breakfast. For me that is a crime. It would be better not to talk at all. I will believe the person who owns virtually nothing and who gives his last possessions to the beggar on the street without telling anyone about it; *he* is saving the world. And he is doing much more than someone who organizes a meeting as a result of hunger in Ethiopia. That is where I see a difference between *word* and *deed*.

We suffer from the fact that our words have lost their meaning. Steiner wrote about that too, that our language is not yet a *real* language. ... Demagogy is the worst sickness of the present time: trickery, empty talk. People's deeds are the deciding factor, not their words—my hero's deed is so absurd that the average person simply cannot decide what the deed consists of. To me, it consists in the fact that babble already disgusts him, that he goes from words to deeds.

NF: And it makes no difference whether or not society records this?

AT: That makes no difference. That is precisely the issue. You know the notion of charity in the gospel. If you give alms, nobody should see it or learn of it if at all possible. Even though pride could also play a role in that. You could think, "Look, I am giving you alms, nobody knows it, but it puts me to rest, I am a morally superior being." So it's not at all easy to be good ... to *appear good is* easy, but to be *truly* good is incredibly difficult.

Love and Fear*

Georg Kühlewind

We have trouble understanding the Old and New Testaments partly because so many of the words there refer to ideas that are now lost to us. Such ideas cannot be approached by ordinary thoughts; they require a higher level of understanding. Take, for example, this pivotal sentence from the First Letter of St. John (4:18):

> There is no fear in love, but perfect love casts out fear. For fear is mutilation,[1] and whoever fears is not perfected in love.

If the ideas behind this sentence were fully understood, it could serve as the foundation for a spiritual psychology.

For St. John, the world and the higher—spiritual—human being were an indivisible unity, a unity made up of three principles or realities. These three realities are, in order of their rank (starting with the highest): Primal Beginning, Grace, and Truth, *Arché, Cháris, and Alétheia*.

The word *Alétheia* is usually translated as *truth*, but we no longer know what John meant by truth. Today, truth means "correctness," in the sense that something coincides with something else: for example, perception with theory. But *Alétheia*[2] means "un-hiddenness"; the state of being "unconcealed," "un-forgotten," "not lost"; it corresponds to living thinking—thinking experienced as a living process. Ordinarily this process happens superconsciously,[3] after which only the resulting finished thoughts appear on the level of everyday consciousness. *Alétheia* is imaginative thinking: thinking that has not yet been reduced to

---

*Georg Kühlewind. *Liebe und Furcht*, unpublished German manuscript, 1988. Trans. Friedemann Schwarzkopf. Re-edited by GK and KF for this volume. Numbered footnotes by the author, asterisk footnotes by the translator.

mirrored, past thinking, representing or perceiving. We *touch* this super-conscious level of the spirit in every new understanding and intuition. To *experience Alétheia* is to *remain* within this lightning-flash of spirit. It is not a final truth; it is the way and it is life, as experience, progressing from unhiddenness to unhiddenness. "Life," in this case, means being present, in the present, in an unforgotten process. *Alétheia* should be conceived in such a way that the expressions "doing the truth" (John 3:21; 1. John 1:6), "being of the truth" (John 18:37; 1. John 3:19), and "knowing that no lie is of the truth" (1. John 2:21) become meaningful.

Love or *Agápe* can serve as a feeling-concept for the reality we call grace (*Cháris*). *Agápe*, as the new commandment, asks "something more" than the old law: "love your neighbor as yourself" (Lev. 19:18). The new "law" is: "love one another even as I have loved you" (John 13:34; 15:12). We hear the same voice in the Sermon on the Mount (Matt. 5) prescribing a love that asks nothing in return, a love without qualifications or conditions, without self-interest. The death on the cross makes justifications and comparisons irrelevant and absurd: "love thy enemies." *Cháris*, the divine reality which pours over into the world of human beings, is similarly portrayed (Luke 6:32-38): "If you love those who love you, what kind of *Cháris* do you have?" The servant who merely follows orders is an unworthy servant (Luke 17:9-10).

Both *Cháris* and *Agápe* point to an abundance which is naturally given in the divine world; both decrease as the hierarchy of existence decreases. In the world of humanity, however, *Cháris* and *Agápe* are realities which have to overcome obstacles—obstacles originating in the human being. By taking the path through the human being, a path in which obstacles must be overcome, divine love (the "first" love, Rev. 2:4, 1. John 4:19) turns into earthly love, the "second" love, the ideal of earthly development. Bear in mind that love, like light, is not an attribute or activity of the gods but their very form of existence (1. John 1:5; 4:16-17).

> This is the message we have heard from him and proclaim to you, that God is light and in him is no darkness.

> God is love, and whoever abides in love abides in God, and God abides in him. In this is love perfected.

Portrait of Georg Kühlewind by Dan Marshall

Human beings can take part in this divine existence. The ideal code of conduct would be to act only out of moral intuition (the new "law" of love), adapting it to present needs and circumstances through moral imagination, and putting it into practice through moral technique. Humanity could live in love: earth was created for this very purpose, to bring about the possibiity of love despite bodily existence and its requirements, an existence which the angels were spared and which remains outside their experience.

Divine and human existence are connected through the common principle of "Primal Beginning," *Arché*. *Arché* is the capacity to create out of nothing, to act without given causes or purposes, the ability to begin or interrupt a chain of causes—to forgive, for instance, or to practice mercy instead of revenge. *Alétheia* and *Cháris* are contained within *Arché*, as Imagination and Inspiration are contained in Intuition. *Arché* is the essential kernel, the star of the human being, the principle which remains after bodily death and which strives in the next incarnation to work in the earthly world through *Cháris* and *Alétheia*. Forces of growth are concealed within *Arché*, out of which love pours and from which the light and self-experience of *Alétheia* continuously come into being. *Alétheia* has passed through concealment, through forgetting. *Cháris* actively penetrates earthly darkness, the lack of understanding. *Arché* is absolute beginning, the ability to grow beyond itself (otherwise it would not be *beginning*); it is abundance as such; whereas *Cháris* consists of pure "overflowing."

The capacity to *begin* and grow (or overflow) is the essence—or rather the *being*—of I-beings, for I-beings are Logos-beings. "In the beginning was the Logos." (John 1:1). The Greek word translated as "was"* in this sentence does not allow a temporal interpretation of "primal beginning." The Logos is the kernel or driving force of *Arché*; in divine creation, as well as in human beginning, the Logos, the capacity to create and grasp meaning, must always be present. The Logos is the structuring principle of the world and humanity, the predisposition for the word and for the ability to speak, think and love in a human sense (*bene velle*—to wish the other well). Therefore, "keeping" or "following" the logos or the logoi of the Lord (John 14:23-24; 8:5) is the precondition for love of the divine, or identical with it, and thus identical with eternal life (1. John 2:5):

> ... but whoever keeps his [the Logos'] word, in him love of God is truly perfected.

Arché is the essence of divine human existence. (The Letter of Jude— Jude 6— states: ". . . the angels who did not keep their own *Arché*."**) And the essence of *Arché* is the Logos. Heraclitus says: "The Logos, which is innate to the soul, grows from out of itself."

Now we can look again at the sentence quoted in the opening paragraph:

> There is no fear in love, but perfect love casts out fear. For fear is mutilation, and whoever fears is not perfected in love.

The words *teleiotes* (perfected), *teleios* (perfect), and *teleioun* (to become perfected) are related to *end* but also to *fulfillment, completion, culmination, dedication, initiation (telos)*. In the context of the sentence quoted above, "perfect love" refers to the full reality of the human being and the world. The *first* does not exist unless creation continues in the world, and the *last* does not exist and is not fulfilled unless human beings continue creation. For within the created world, only the human being can

---

* The original Greek uses "was," which is *im-perfect*, i.e., the unfinished, uncompleted past—in contradistinction to the perfect, accomplished past— "has been," which means that beginning in the Logos always *was, still is*, and continues to *be*.

** Luther translates Arché as "principality," the Revised Standard Version as "position," the King James Version as "first estate."

continue creation, and within that world, only the human being represents the living Logos. Thus one reads in St. Paul's Letter to the Romans (8:19, 22):

> For the creation waits with eager longing for the manifestation of the sons of God. ... Because we know that everything created has been groaning and is still in fear from the beginning until now.

The initiate (the "perfected," *teleios*) is a human being through whom the original spiritual nature of *Arché*—and, through *Arché*, also *Cháris* and *Alétheia*—can be manifested on *earth*. The attribute of abundance is brought up immediately after the Sermon on the Mount, when such unheard-of admonitions as (Matt. 5:39)—"For if you love those who love you, what reward have you?"—are followed by the words: "You therefore must be perfect. ..." (Matt. 5:46) Finally the rich youth is told: "If you would be perfect, go, sell what you possess and give to the poor, and you will have treasure in the heavens ..." (Matt. 19:21). And in Revelations, immediately after the Logos-Being says "I am the Alpha and the Omega, the beginning and the completion."* (Rev. 21:6; 22:13), an example of *Cháris* is given: "To the thirsty I will give from the fountain of the water of life *without recompense*." (Rev. 21:6)

Perfection is the manifestation of what is predisposed in *Arché*: over-abundant complete love on the level of feeling. To quote St. Paul again:

> Now, draw towards yourselves... over and above all else, love, the bond of perfectedness. (Col. 3:14)

Wherever there is true beginning, there is love, and without beginning there is no love; and in the primal beginning was the Logos.

The hymn to love in St. Paul's First Letter to the Corinthians (Cor. 13) culminates in the description of the arrival of the "perfected one." This chapter is the description of the Logos-Being in the light of love. Without love, the human being becomes a plaything of other forces and cannot sustain itself as an I-being. *Arché*, *Cháris* and *Alétheia* are the forms of existence of I-beings: "The I-am is the beginning and the completion"— *completion* in the sense mentioned above. All three forms of existence

---

* which is usually translated as "end" (telos).

imply continuous growing and increasing as well as: unfinished-ness. This kind of growth, this creation out of nothing, is unknown to modern scientific thinking, which only investigates the already-created, the past or result of creation, the world of the laws of the preservation of energy and matter.

This sort of growth can be suppressed in various ways, most of whose causes can be found within the human being. When growth is obstructed, there is the feeling of fear, the opposite of the spiritual "I-am" experience that occurs during growth. Fear is the feeling of "I-am-not" and occurs when growth is denied, lacking, or diminished. In this sense, fear is mutilation. The I-am lives—exists, is in *surrender*—in creation and love. Dedication, receptive attention, the reversed, *receiving will*,[4] the aim and essence of every meditation, hold the possibility of a transformation of the I (or the attention) into that which the I knows, or *cognizes*, a transmutation experienced by the knower. I know *that* by experiencing my own metamorphosis into *that*.

For ordinary logic it makes no difference whether one says "I am you" or "You are I." But in reality these are two different movements. Rudolf Steiner states:

> While it's true that in super-sensible consciousness the human soul awakens within the spiritual world, it's also true that, in love, the spiritual awakens within the sense-perceptible world. [5]

This statement might be compared with the passages cited earlier (1. John 1:5; John 4:16).

I cannot transform myself into another I-being because an I-being has no finished existence; it is not merely a creature, result, product, but is itself in the process of creating; it is itself a source. One can transform oneself into something that is completed, whereas a formative *source* (Gestalt-Quelle), Logos-source, word-source, can only be *received* into oneself.

In the sense-perceptible physical world, love is the supernatural "law" or commandment. If the spirit remains true to its essential nature, it creates something above and beyond Nature when it appears as love in the sense-perceptible realm. Love is the extinction of one's own I-force by the use of that very I-force: for the sake of the other. For this to occur, the other is needed, and an other exists—in reality—only in the sense-perceptible world. The other remains an other for love—I surrender myself; I become the other by letting him "in." In this way the sense-perceptible world—otherwise completed—gains perfection or wholeness; the continuing power of creation enters the sense-perceptible world through the Logos-force of love. For

> where two or three are gathered in my name, there am I in the midst of them. (Matt. 18:20)

In the center of every single human being shines the Logos, and thus it is also among them. It is the Logos[6] who unites I-beings.

Notes

1. The Greek word *kólasis*, which Luther translates as *pain*, *suffering*, and which the Revised Standard Version translates as *punishment*, stems from the Greek verb *Kolázzo*, which originally meant the pruning of superfluous parts of trees and plants. In a metaphorical sense the word means "punishing," "chastising," hence also "pain."

2. About *Alétheia* and *Cháris*, see Georg Kühlewind, *Becoming Aware of the Logos*, Chap. 10 (Great Barrington, MA: Lindisfarne Press, 1985).

3. Georg Kühlewind, *Stages of Consciousness*. "The Two Levels of Consciousness in *The Philosophy of Freedom*," (Great Barrington, MA: Lindisfarne Press, 1984).

4. Rudolf Steiner *Vom Menschenrälsel*, "Ausblicke." (Dornach, Switzerland: Rudolf Steiner Verlag, 1957) (GA 20). Georg Kühlewind, "The Reversal of the Will and the Encounter with the Logos-force," *Schooling of Consciousness*. Trans. Friedmann Schwarzkopf (Fair Oaks, CA: Rudolf Steiner College Publications, 1986).

5. Rudolf Steiner. *Die Schwelle der geistigen Welt*, "Von dem Ich-Gefühl und der Liebefähigkeit" (Dornach, Switzerland: Rudolf Steiner Verlag, 1972) (GA 17).

6. In the Bible—as in every living text—words are never unambiguous. Whether words such as *Logos* or *Arché* are used in their deepest or in their everyday sense has to be explored in each case. Often the meaning has to be found on several levels, which gives the text its peculiar coloring. In the profoundest texts, words are used in their primal sense, which allows for every possible meaning. In such a case, the meaning cannot be "explained" or defined; it corresponds to the unreduceable original intuition of the respective word.

Search for a Still Point: *Humboldt's Gift*

Nick Lyons

Humboldt's Gift by Saul Bellow (New York: Viking Press, 1975), 487 pages.

Toward the end of Saul Bellow's *The Adventures of Augie March*, Augie says with uncommon conviction that he has a "feeling about the axial lines of life, with respect to which you must be straight or else your existence is merely clownery, hiding tragedy." Someone on such axial lines has "truth, love, peace, bounty, usefulness, harmony," and all "noise and grates, distortion, chatter, distraction, effort, superfluity," pass off like something unreal. Such has been the goal of all Bellow's heroes: Joseph (the "dangling man"), Asa Leventhal (the "victim"). Augie, Tommy Wilhelm (in *Seize the Day*), the abundant Henderson (the "rain king"), Herzog, and the bewildered Sammler all seek and would wish to be judged by these yardsticks. Bellow's first novels demonstrate a cycle of consistent growth toward such axial lines—registering an anguish, exuberance, whimsy, pathos, comedy, and painfully honest groping in which he cheats neither the complexities of the personal life nor the ambiguities of our moment in American history.

"At any time," Augie says, "life can come together again and man be regenerated . . . the man himself, finite and trapped as he is, can live, where the axial lines are." That was said twenty years ago. Such has been Bellow's search—in novels that, seesawing, and with increased profundity, have explored lives hemmed in by their fears and failures, by the discrete calls of flesh and mind, by the need for independence and the need to unite. It is thus no shock (though most critics have taken it as such) that in his eighth novel, *Humboldt's Gift*, Bellow, perhaps America's most thoughtful novelist, should have a central figure, Charles Citrine, "discover" anthroposophy. By other names, and through other characters, he may have been searching for it all along.

Certainly, the anthroposophy in this new and important (if not entirely successful) novel is only fragmentary: Bellow focuses almost exclusively on meditation exercises outlined in *Knowledge of the Higher Worlds and Its Attainment*. Citrine, a prominent and publicly successful intellectual living in Chicago, is besieged by memories of his dead friend and literary mentor, one Humboldt Fleisher (a brilliant, tormented poet, based loosely on the late Delmore Schwartz), a gnashing settlement with his ex-wife, financial woes and broad philosophical doubts, and a humorous and persistent entanglement with a small-time criminal named Cantabile. A Professor Scheldt gives Citrine some of Rudolf Steiner's books and lectures, and talks patiently with him about certain basic concepts. Through Scheldt, Bellow reveals his own deft novelist's understanding. After Citrine has spoken of Steiner's ideas, and has asked Scheldt whether he has properly understood them, the old professor— his face "interested and plain"—says: "All this is in the texts. I can't be sure that you have grasped it all but you're fairly accurate." Though Citrine's friends tell him anthroposophy is a sham or madness, he has found in his meditations a truth and consolation, the beginnings of an understanding about death, a still point he has been seeking all his life. As an "intellectual," he has begun to learn it first in his head, but the book ends and he vows to visit the Goetheanum; anthroposophy is becoming more of a working force in his life.

A novelist's first obligation is to the truth of his art. Bellow is making no plea for anthroposophy, nor is he attempting to present it in all its dimensions. The meditation exercises, fairly plucked—though indeed *plucked*—from *Knowledge of the Higher Worlds*, serve distinct functions in the novel: they enable Citrine to recall his dead friend with patient, objective clarity, and they provide him with a still point in the midst of his personal chaos. The man is being torn apart by threats and betrayals from within and from without, and anthroposophy becomes his chief line of defense. Fair enough. Though the anthroposophy is a bit lumpy in the novel, and the novel is somehow too discursive (there's *so* much talk—and *must* Citrine have an affair with Scheldt's daughter and take that tiresome trip to Texas?), even prolix, what we have is brilliant and honest. The book warrants the widest possible reading.

One intriguing upshot of its publication has been the reactions of the reviewers. One "generously" says he is unwilling to call Steiner "a quack"; another speaks of the Steiner "farrago" as being merely a metaphor for the creative imagination; several obviously had to look up anthroposophy in encyclopedias, and got little further than hollow definitions; others refer to it as merely mysticism and imply that Bellow has gone soft.

But Bellow was obviously sincere in his use of anthroposophy. In a *Newsweek* interview he said he has been "impressed by the idea that there were forms of understanding, discredited now, which had long been the agreed basis of human knowledge. We think we can know the world scientifically, but actually our ignorance is terrifying." On a recent trip to England he intended to talk with Owen Barfield, whose *Saving the Appearances* had deeply impressed him.

Surely the greatest part of Von Humboldt Fleisher's legacy and gift, beyond the screen scripts that are financially rewarding to Citrine, is his closing assertion in a letter: "Remember: we are not natural beings but supernatural beings." Citrine accepts this, too, suggesting that Bellow has moved steadily from his view of man as "finite" to a spiritual view of man that alone can put human beings on "the axial lines of life."

This may be Bellow's greatest gift, too: he has reminded American "intellectuals" that they are not mere thinkers but have unused powers of perception—and that there is a path, long ignored and even mocked, called anthroposophy (which his Citrine has not yet fully grasped but begun to appreciate) that just might be worth their patient study.

Psychoanalysis and Anthroposophy*

Michael Lipson

Anthroposophy and psychoanalysis derive from the lifework of two Austrian near-contemporaries, Rudolf Steiner (1861-1925) and Sigmund Freud (1859-1938), and the movements they founded remain inescapably tied to the two men. Both attempted to reconcile the non-rational foundations of human consciousness with Western natural science. Both regarded human society and individuals at the turn of the century as psychically sick, and both proposed cures particularly apt, they thought, for the people of our time to embrace. The work of both, in its aim at self-conscious and self-directed liberation of each individual, was persecuted by followers of another 20th-century Austrian, Adolf Hitler.

Freud's legacy has enjoyed an unparalleled cultural ascendancy since his death, so that all biography, literature, philosophy and psychology bear to some degree the stamp of the psychoanalytic worldview. Steiner lamented as early as in his lectures of the 19-teens on psychoanalysis that the time is over when a young girl can kiss her father without it being taken as a sexual event (cf. Steiner, *Psychoanalysis and Spiritual Psychology*, Hudson, NY: Anthroposophical Press, 1990). Steiner's work and the fruits of the anthroposophical movement have remained far less known, less culturally nameable, less obviously pervasive. Something has changed fundamentally because Steiner developed anthroposophy, but it has not succeeded as the cultural movement he intended it to be.

Psychoanalysis has been largely supplanted in the world of psychotherapy by many other schools, yet it retains a special status as their common technical ancestor and in its pretension to explain the whole of human

* Revised by the author from a talk given in Great Barrington, MA, September 1994.

functioning and cultural history. Steiner's critique of psychoanalysis in the 'teens still applies, with much validity, not only to today's psychoanalysis but to the range of cognitive-behavioral, body-centered, and even "transpersonal" therapies of our time. By comparing anthroposophy to psychoanalysis, I am also comparing it to all psychologies in their fallen state—even to anthroposophy.

Freud started from dream. His 1899 *Interpretation of Dreams*, especially its dense seventh chapter, contains in embryo the whole of his later works. The dream, for Freud, is only partly known. In the morning, we recall the "manifest" dream, and must guess our way back to the "latent" dream—itself never directly available to waking consciousness—through our interpretation of the dream's images. When we do so, we find that the dream always expresses a wish, to which it (partially) accords the satisfaction denied in waking life. For the wishes are often sexual or aggressive—at any rate, they run counter to social or personal norms. The remembered dream allows for partial release of a drive, a biologically rooted impulse, whose operations have been pushed out of consciousness because they are unacceptable. The work of psychoanalysis is to allow fully into waking consciousness the conceptual contents, though, as we said, never the direct current experience, contained in the dream.

Steiner takes his start not from dream, but from thinking. In his 1894 *Philosophy of Freedom*, he focuses not on a finished content from the recent psychic past—such as the daytime psychic events, pushed out of awareness, that give rise to the Freudian dream—but rather on the current, active process of thinking itself. Thinking is not a memory of something that happened (cf. Freud in *Studies on Hysteria*, 1899): "Our hysterical patients suffer from reminiscences," but is something we are currently creating. His earliest works are an epistemological series taking their sustenance (not their source) from the scientific writings of Goethe that Steiner was called on to edit while still in his early twenties.

While Freud began as a medical doctor facing quasi-physical ailments in patients who were to be named, in the psychoanalytic literature, only by confidential pseudonyms (e.g., "Anna von O"), Steiner began with the philosophy and science of the German-speaking world's most exemplary, most nameable thinker, Johann Wolfgang von Goethe, and with the healthy foundation of ideas. Since Freud's work began with the treatment of illness, the dream was theorized on the model of psychoneurotic symptoms. It was always and essentially conflictual, representing a final outcome of the battle between (ultimately) the body's wishes and our parents' commands. Steiner, by contrast, was concerned to describe the nature of healthy thinking and perceiving, a "conflict-free" sphere, as the generation of Ego Psychologists would have called it. Even more: when he focused on thinking, it was not ordinary thinking which Steiner celebrated, but a healthy (and therefore highly abnormal) thinking—a "living" thinking that stands in relation to our normal waking life and our normal (e.g., scientific) thinking as this stands in relation to dreaming (see in this connection Otto Palmer, *Rudolf Steiner on his Book, The Philosophy of Freedom*, 1975). For Freud, there is no higher rationality than that of scientific thinking, and this is itself a mixed blessing, being won at the cost of our more real, earthier selves.

The psychoanalytic method Freud developed (with Breuer and their creative patient Bertha von Pappenheim) attempted to replicate the state of dreaming. The patient was to state what came to mind freely, relaxing the censorship of socially unacceptable contents, and so be led by the ever invisible unconscious to areas of conflict, there to work them through and out by this very act of verbalizing and rendering them conscious—also rendering them interpersonal, as later analysts would note. The recumbent attitude on the psychoanalytic couch, a holdover from mesmerist practices, was meant to encourage a prelogical relaxation of conscious mental control. The dreamer's translation of primitive emotional contents into verbal and imagistic expression in the dream corresponds to the recumbent patient's intentionally relaxed, "freely associative" speech on the couch. As the manifest dream had to be interpreted back to its original latent form, so the associate chain of the patient's speech had to be interpreted back to its instinctual or conflictive roots.

Steiner's methods lead in the exactly opposite direction, away from dreaming toward heightened waking. The clarity, self-direction, and cogency that characterize waking thought, as compared with dream-thought, are redoubled in that activity he calls, with misleading, insistent phenomenological simplicity, "thinking." In psychoanalytic theory, waking thought appears as something like an evasion of the truer reality that is sublogical, biological, primitive, sexual and aggressive; anthroposophical research finds normal waking thought to be the lowest derivative of a truer reality that is logical, spiritual, creative, uncreated and loving. The "attention" in Steiner is an infinitely directable, teachable faculty. It is who we are, and through it we are, potentially, everything. In Freud, the attention appears under a different name as "libido," and attaches primarily to the physical body.

We could follow these comparisons even into myth—though of course their expression in myth does not increase their legitimacy. For example, whereas Wolfram von Eschenbach's Parzival throws down his reins on the neck of the Grail-steed to be led by this divine beast to the scene of the Grail, Freud has the ego, the puny waking self, throw down its reins on the neck of the stallion of its own biological life to find its proper way (the image can be found in Freud's 1923 *The Ego and the Id*). The key difference here is not easy to see. For it is not only a different inner agent, but a different kind of agent and gesture altogether. Freud and Jung alike advocate a lowering of the mental level to attain a truer self; in Steiner, what corresponds to throwing one's reins onto the Grail-steed's neck actually entails an unusually constituted increase in the level of cognitive clarity and strength of will.

Steiner's orientation is always toward a future state perceived as good, while Freud wants to emphasize a past state that may well be unsavory by adult Western standards. The "future" and "past" being referred to here are both individual/cognitive and anthropological/historical. They did very different things with the same Darwin and Haeckel. Steiner was interested in the benevolent future of the human species as being, in principal, of unlimited potential for transformation and creativity. And this "future" is potentially available and present to each person in each act of cognition, of knowing. This kind of future is return with a difference: the spiritual worlds, in which we lived as infants and as an infant species, and from which we benefited without knowing of them, we will reinvent and reinhabit. For Freud, the "past" of the species, when we were more openly hostile and sexual, is also the past of any

Rudolf Steiner   *Sigmund Freud*

individual, who recapitulates it in infancy and only gradually submits to the structure of society. The development of the Freudian adult, then, is also return with a difference: toward relaxed censorship of "primitive," earthy drives and toward their integration into adaptive social functioning. Both thinkers look to a final state that recapitulates the originary, but with an increase in individual self-awareness.

Steiner noted that our ordinary life of thought is like a field of corpses, and the healthy response at seeing this is to seek the actual life of thinking from which these corpses have been sundered. The corpses (our finished thoughts of the normal kind) have already become; they are of the past in this sense; they are dead. The life-in-thinking (or perceiving, etc.) that one seeks is not of the past, nor even of the present, but ultimately of the currently-experienced future. To live it is therefore to step outside the ordinary flow of time. Psychoanalysis knows nothing of this kind of past or this kind of future.

When Steiner criticized psychoanalysis, he tellingly included Jung with Freud, though Jung had already broken with Freud at the time. For

Steiner, the essential problem with Freud was the inadequate cognitive means by which very real areas of human life are addressed. Jung's archetypes and symbols stem from no higher cognitive level than Freud's "neuroses," as a close reading of his *Memories, Dreams and Reflections* makes clear. If anything, the sense for the real is weaker in Jung.

For it is not the apparent content of our insights that matters, but rather the quality, the intensity, of our involvement. "Our science is a substitute for our religion," remarked T. S. Eliot, "and so is our religion." What matters is not whether we say "phallic stage," (Freud) or "anima," (Jung) or "etheric body," (Steiner), but the level of cognition we bring to bear. We do not understand a life by arranging it in seven-year cycles, any more than we understand it by linking adult to childhood psychosexual conflicts. A person's real life is the life experienced meditatively, or recalled meditatively—in other words, as Emerson pointed out, "a very few moments."

Steiner was far from considering sexuality unimportant, nor was he squeamish about it. But its essential reduction to animality and lust, the assumption that we know what it is and need either simply to celebrate it or catalogue our evasions from it—this psychoanalytic style was very far from Steiner's. There was no allowance in Freud, nor is there in most of the schools of psychology today, for the idea that sexuality might be much more than we imagine or can perceive with normal consciousness.

Freud became increasingly pessimistic over the years as to the curative potential of psychoanalysis; Steiner always maintained that every human being (not just the "analyzable" or higher-functioning ones) has the potential, with time and work, to transform themselves radically. In a famous passage in the early *Studies on Hysteria*, Freud grimly claims that "much will have been achieved" if a patient's "neurotic misery" can be changed into "ordinary unhappiness." Here is Steiner in *Knowledge of the Higher Worlds and Its Attainment*, Chapter 10: "It is given to us to perfect ourselves, in time to transform ourselves utterly. But this transformation must take place in our innermost nature, in our life of thought."

We could go on contrasting aspects of Freud with aspects of Steiner, but I would like to pause and consider just how similar they are from a certain standpoint. At the beginning of the last century, both men founded movements that sought, with great ambition, to explain the whole of human life, accounting not only for local, modern, Western history, but for the human being as such. Their totalizing systems have tended to attract fervent followers who cannot, of their own experience, confirm what the Master said but who preach the truths they have received. Both were eager for humans to change themselves on the basis of individual insight, an outrageous project by the standards of earlier civilizations. Freud's letters have revealed that he was quite fascinated by psychic experience, even in such areas as precognition, but he always stayed away from them in his written works, aiming as he did at scientific respectability. Here and there, for example, in his letters to his friend Fliess, in his repeated flirtation with psychic phenomena, and at moments in his published works (e.g., in *Civilization and its Discontents, The Future of an Illusion, Moses and Monotheism*), we glimpse his yearning for a transcendence he feels compelled to deny. We can also recall the anecdote in Jung's memoirs in which he reports Freud as saying that the sexual etiology of neurosis is the only defense against the "black tide of mud" of occultism.

Looking at their affinity from the other direction, we can notice that, though Steiner often referred favorably to the world's religions present and past while Freud analyzed, the better to dismiss them, Steiner actually was thoroughly modern, even postmodern, in his rejection of received religious dogma. His early works, especially the scorching "Egotism and Philosophy" of 1899, attempt to root out the reliance on any extra-human source of certainty, authority or truth. Like Freud, then, Steiner participated in the very 20th-century notion, close to the heart of the best Western science, that it is up to each contemporary soul to achieve its own understanding and to base its actions accordingly.

Yet—and here we come back to contrasts—Steiner and Freud differed fundamentally on the question of the nature of the reality to be sought and the conditions of its knowing. Freud, like the natural scientists of his day and our own, was thoroughly Kantian. That is, he based his theories on the idea that we cannot know directly the source of our world, nor of our own consciousness. In Freud, the sources for dreams, symptoms, and all the more so for art and creativity, lie in the realm of the to-be guessed-at, the to-be-deduced. We look at clues, follow a trail, and may triumphantly declare that we have found the perpetrator of our mental life: a quasi-physical "drive" or its "derivatives." For Steiner there is, in principle, nothing hidden. He says of himself in *The Course of My Life* that at a certain period he made sure not to be influenced by harmful forces, "not even unconsciously." In the post-Freudian world we have to wonder how he can be sure of that. If we thought anyone really could be sure, it would present a far greater challenge to our worldview than anything in psychoanalysis or the entire range of psychotherapies that exist today.

According to the anthroposophical view, we can meet everything and any being directly if we will only transform our cognitive powers adequately. The Kantian stance forgoes this intimacy but gains in fixity: I may not be able directly to experience the ground of my world, the source of the qualities familiar to me, but at least I know they are fixed and there—unalterably present whether I perceive them or not. In the Steinerian view, a view to which science and philosophy are gradually, though only superficially, acceding, there is no "outer reality." We have rather a world of meanings in which we ourselves participate.

Both thinkers were shocking in their day for declaring that the familiar psychic world actually conceals a world that is much more eloquent, that speaks, that has significance in every part. This is reflected for example in the (little) psychoanalytic joke: one analyst passes a colleague on the street; the colleague says, "Hi, how are you?" and afterwards the first analyst mutters to himself, "I wonder what he meant by that?" Freud was well aware that he saw meaning where others saw insignificant jokes, meaningless errors, or chance acts. For Freud, every utterance, indeed every human activity, is significant. The meanings in question, as we have seen, tend to be relatively unacceptable socially, relatively primitive, relatively earthy or biologically based. When he quoted the Scholastic motto, *saxa loquuntur*, "the stones speak," he meant that the apparently inert symptoms of hysteria, for example, could be made to submit to analysis and yield a fruit of "meaning": e.g., that a young woman secretly wished her ill father dead.

Steiner's "meanings" are of a different order. Where a symptom means something *else* for Freud, something at which we must guess, to Steiner a tree or a stone means *itself*. As we first see it, it is the misunderstood aspect of a sacred meaning. Its very physicality is such a meaning, not an outward "thing," other than and foreign to us. Freud would have us ignore the physical world and debunk the social world, rendering them more and more profane; Steiner's training in cognition would have us know these worlds as holy and make more.

In psychoanalysis, which has at times had pretensions to being a general psychology, there is remarkably little to be said about the physical world. Its understanding is presumed to come from natural science as currently constituted. In anthroposophy, there is the assertion that we do not really know the physical world at all, unless we develop our cognitive capacities in a profound and unaccustomed way. What we then find is not, as for natural science, inferential knowledge of smaller and smaller things out there (atoms, particles, forces) but deeper and deeper meanings in which we ourselves are intimately implicated. This intimacy of cognition in Steiner—and cognition of the world, of every pebble, blade of grass, owl and spiritual being—has as its impoverished correlative in Freud only a suspicion of states of "merger" as primitive if not pathological.

And yet, while my list of contrasts to the advantage of anthroposophy threatens to grow infinite (we could, for example, add the importance of the analyst to Freud's patients as a source of insight and relationship, and set against it Steiner's warnings—with respect to psychoanalysis itself and adult schooling generally—that the student's own efforts and nonprofessional relationships are the decisive factor) there is at least one great benefit from psychoanalysis that is perhaps less salient in anthroposophy. I am thinking of actual effort to transform speech. Where anthroposophists may prattle about the results of spiritual scientific research, Freudians and their therapeutic descendants actually engage in the "research" of psychotherapy. There is therefore an emphasis on continual current practice of the highest forms of interpersonal knowing available. The psychoanalytic forms are certainly inadequate, but on the other hand they are continually changing.

Anthroposophy has tended to follow gradually after Steiner's "indications" in a number of fields, rarely or never claiming to attain the summit, or even the lower foothills, of his cognitive achievements. Psychoanalysts have perhaps been emboldened by the relative humbleness of their own Sage's achievements, for all these are overglorified, and so they have not only actually practiced his methods, but made so bold as continually to improve them.

Thus, the original Freudian detective hunt for repressed memories of trauma, the pin-the-tail-on-the-donkey matching of symptoms to their antecedents or assumed "meanings," has given way to a myriad of techniques and styles in current psychoanalysis. The emphasis on developing a real and supportive relationship with the analyst, which would have shocked first- or second-generation analysts, is now commonplace, as is the view that it is the interactive process, not the insight into "contents," that is curative. The idea of analysis as verbal play, leading to spontaneity and creativity, has emerged and flourished in part as a result of the innovations of D.W. Winnicott in the sixties and seventies. Feminist psychoanalysis has questioned and rewritten many of the basic tenets of early Freudianism, attempting to undo some of its power relations, chauvinism, and epistemological naiveté. In all this, psychoanalysis has moved with the cultural currents of our century. Dare anthroposophy point to Steiner's mistakes and show how it has moved beyond them? Or is it still prey to hero-worship, timidity, traditionalism, lack of exercise?

The possible anthroposophical objection here, that after all Freud's achievements can be surveyed, and therefore improved upon, while Steiner's continue to lie outside our range of perception, is only partially valid. The anthroposophical movement has perhaps been misled by the wealth of its legacy from Steiner. We have so many directions to pursue, in agriculture, in education, in arts, in social development, in inner work. We have Steiner's writings and thousands of lectures. We have the work of many great anthroposophists. Perhaps we therefore forget what is most important for growth: our moment-to-moment poverty (though this alone is the condition for attainment, celebrated in the Beatitudes of the Sermon on the Mount). At least the psychoanalytic worldview, world-weary and suspicious of easy consolation, remains close to the poverty of 20th-century experience, a stark experience of the cruelty, uselessness, repetitiveness, selfishness and ignorance that characterize so much of our lives.

Having less august goals and less rosy hopes, psychoanalysis tends to confront people with the meanness of life, and in the right hands this can become a spur to action. They are the right hands when, in spite of a materialist worldview, an analyst manages to bring the patient's awareness to a higher pitch of intensity, and so to bring forth that which recognizes the meanness and so is other than it. As Keats wrote in "What the Thrush Said," "He who saddens / At thought of idleness cannot be idle, / And he's awake who thinks himself asleep." We can note, in this connection, the striking passage in the traditional psychoanalyst I.H. Paul's *Letters to Simon* (1972), in his description of the practice of "impassive listening": "… it gave the sessions a quality they didn't have before; it generally made a significant difference in the way my patient spoke. He still spoke to me (and when I felt he didn't I was quick to comment on that), but at the same time he also spoke to himself. At times, it was as if part of him was listening in the same way that I was listening. At such times, there was an almost uncanny sense that there were three of us in the room."

Anthroposophy, with its killingly good answers to fundamental questions, its totalizing view, its great Master, and its spiritual worlds waiting for our participation, in the wrong hands can tend to cast a spun-sugar curtain over our necessary experience of emptiness, and cast up another Kantian otherness just when we need to undo the old one. By the "wrong hands," I mean my own hands—or anyone's at those (perhaps inevitable) moments when we forget that the spiritual worlds are ours to create, not ours to have.

To advance on the path of spiritual research is to advance: to experience, to go through something and know we are doing so. For this to happen we must also make moral advances, and really see ourselves in our maculate variety. How much effort is really put into seeing our interpersonal foibles, our held-over angers, pettiness, jealousy, pride and lust? Yet these unglamorous, essential lessons are staples of psychoanalytic practice, whose practitioners have also striven to avoid moralistic shaming of the patient.

In his early *Knowledge of the Higher Worlds and Its Attainment* (1904/5), Steiner conjures up the image of the Guardian of the Threshold, part of whose mission is to confront us with our failings and incompleteness. While anthroposophists await the stunning vision of this awesome entity, perhaps eager to endure a salutary and interesting trial, psychoanalysts may prompt their patients actually to achieve key aspects of the encounter. For its meaning is not primarily, "I saw a spiritual being!" but rather (in part), "I am jealous, selfish, deceitful, vengeful, stupid, proud," (and, we must add) "*etc.*"

Some years ago, the educator David Spangler, at a conference on the nature of evil, listened patiently to an account of the ornate spiritual healing technique a participant described and then he remarked, "The spiritual worlds are very forgiving. They will fill pretty well any form we care to impose on them." We must ask ourselves whether in psychoanalysis and other epistemologically insufficient psychologies (Gestalt, Jungian, Transpersonal, Bodywork, Eriksonian, Cognitive-Behavioral, Rational-Emotive) some of the spiritual development foregone by anthroposophy has in fact taken place. Why did Dante put the Inferno before the Purgatorio and the Paradiso? The answer to this question also clarifies the usefulness of psychoanalytic issues being fully, repeatedly, even demeaningly brought home though our true home lies in a country unknown to psychoanalysis.

Philology and the Incarnation

Owen Barfield

Sir Thomas Browne, that mystical, or quasi-mystical, author of the seventeenth century, wrote a book which he called *Religio Medici: The Religion of a Doctor, A Medical Man.* Many, many years later—in my own youth, in fact—Professor Gilbert Murray, who is well-known in England and is probably known over here as a Greek scholar and humanist, wrote a little book (or it may have been no more than a single lecture reprinted) called *Religio Grammatici, The Religion of a Scholar, or Man of Letters.* It occurred to me after I had given the title of this lecture, that if I had been a little more pretentious or a little more brash, perhaps I might have ventured to call it *Religio Philologi*, which I suppose would mean "The Religion of a Student of Language," perhaps especially a student of the historical aspect of language.

It is impossible to give much attention to words and their meanings, and more especially the history of words and the history of the changes which those meanings have undergone, without making a number of interesting discoveries. Moreover, in my experience the discoveries one then makes are of a kind which it is impossible to make without being forced by them to reflect rather intensively on the whole nature of man and of the world in which he lives.

Let me give you a very simple example. Has it ever occurred to you, I wonder, that the epithet "charming" as people use the word today, has certain very odd features about it? In the first place, it is the present participle of a verb active, namely the verb "to charm." Grammatically, therefore, when we speak of an object, a garden, for instance, or a landscape, or perhaps a person, as "charming," we make that object or person the subject of a verb which denotes an activity of some sort. That is what we do grammatically, but it is not at all, or it is only very rarely, what we mean semantically. When we speak, for instance, of a child as charming, we do not mean that the child himself is actually doing something. On the contrary, as soon as we notice that anyone, a child or a woman, is "charming" us in the verbal sense (in which case we rarely use the simple verb by itself, but we find some other expression such as "putting on charm" or "exerting charm" so as to bring out the notion of a willed activity), when that happens, the charmer who is charming in the verbal sense generally ceases to be charming in the adjectival sense!

Well, you could say the same thing about the word "enchanting." I mention these two words because they're good examples of a whole class, quite a noticeable group of words in our language which possess the same peculiarity. One has only to think of such words as *depressing, interesting, amusing, entertaining, entrancing, fascinating,* and so on to realize that we tend to allude to qualitative manifestations in the world outside ourselves by describing the effect they have on us, rather than by attempting to denote the qualities themselves.

The next thing that you find about this little group of words, if you go into the matter historically, is that these words, when used with these meanings, are all comparatively recent arrivals. Most of them first came into use in the eighteenth century—none of them is earlier than the seventeenth, I think. The kind of question one is led to ask is: Is this just an accident, or has it any wider significance? That is just the kind of question which the philologist, the student of language in its historical aspect, is led on to ask himself. Is the appearance of these words at this comparatively late stage just something that happened to happen, or is it a surface manifestation of deeper currents of some sort? So you have a linguistic habit, one must say, arising in the West in the course of the last few centuries, of describing or defining or denoting the outer world in terms, as it were, of the inner world of human feeling.

Now, let us take a look at another group of words, a very much larger group this time, indeed an almost unlimited one. I am referring to all those words which go to make up what the nineteenth century utilitarian philosopher Jeremy Bentham called the "immaterial language." In other words, I mean all those innumerable words in any modern language which do not refer to anything in the outside world at all, but only to the inner world of human feeling, of human thought—only to states of mind or mental events—*hope, fear, enthusiasm, conscious, embarrass, humility, ambition, concept*—you can go on reeling them off, any number of them, of course. If you take the trouble to look up the etymologies of these words, you will find that in every case either they or their predecessors in older languages from which we have taken them, at one time referred not only to states of mind or mental events but also to some thing or some event in the outer world; that is of course what one might call elementary etymology. Only this time it is not usually a matter of looking back just a few hundred years into the past. We have to take a much longer survey if we wish to observe the historical process to which I am now seeking to draw your attention.

First, let me make this point—everyone is agreed, and I repeat, *everyone*, that there *was* such a historical process. Now you may ask, How do I establish that rather bold proposition? And the answer is: I establish it because I am in a position to call two witnesses to it from the very opposite ends of the earth. In saying "the opposite ends of the earth," I am not only alluding to the fact that one of them is American and the other is English, though that happens to be the case, but I am thinking much rather of the fact that they represent diametrically opposite philosophies, diametrically opposite points of view and beliefs about the whole nature of man and his relation to the divine disposition in the world. The two witnesses I'm thinking of are the transcendentalist Emerson, and the positivist philosopher to whom I've already referred, Jeremy Bentham. You'll find in the section on language in the longer of Emerson's two essays which are entitled "Nature" the following passage: "Every word used to express a moral or intellectual fact, if traced to its root, is found to be borrowed from material appearance. *Right* means *straight; wrong* means *twisted. Spirit* primarily means *wind; transgression*, the *crossing of a line; supercilious*, the *raising of the eyebrows*. We say *heart* to express emotion, the *head* to denote thought, and *thought* and *emotion* are words borrowed from sensible things, and now appropriated to spiritual nature. Most of the process by which this transformation is made is hidden from us in the remote time when language was formed." Well, that is Emerson.

Then you find Jeremy Bentham, hardheaded positivist Jeremy Bentham, in an essay of his entitled "Language," (it comes in section four of the essay), writing as follows: "Throughout the whole field of language, parallel to the line of what may be termed the material language, and expressed by the same words, runs a line of what may be termed the immaterial language. Not that to every word that has a material import there belongs also an immaterial one; but that to every word that has an immaterial import there belongs, or at least did belong, a material one." When, therefore, we approach this immaterial language, these words which refer to the inner world only, we know that we have to do with words that at one time were words of the material language. We know that there has been a transition from the material language into an immaterial one.

Can we still go further and, at least in some cases, observe the transition taking place? The answer is that in some cases we can. You see, if in the case of any words of the immaterial language, we can lay our finger on a period in its history when the older material meaning had not yet evaporated, if I may put it that way, while the later immaterial meaning had already appeared, then we shall have located the transition itself.

Now let me take one of the examples Emerson himself gives, where he writes: "*Spirit* primarily means *wind*." I imagine that is as good an example as any you could choose of an immaterial meaning which was originally a material one. In this instance we have the best possible evidence that there *was* a particular time when the material meaning and the immaterial meaning still operated side by side in the same word. Not only so, but we know that that time was the time, about the beginning of our era, in which the New Testament was being written. Because in the third chapter of John's gospel you read in the account of our Lord's encounter with Nicodemus, first the words, "That which is born of the flesh is flesh and that which is born of the spirit is spirit." And then, in the next verse, "The wind bloweth where it listeth, and thou hearest the sound thereof, but canst not tell whence it cometh, and whither it goeth." And then again, "So is every one that is born of the Spirit." But in the Greek it is the same word "*pneuma*" that is used, whether it is wind or spirit that is being referred to. In rendering the two phrases, which occur in one and the same verse, "the wind bloweth where it listeth," and "everyone that is born of the Spirit," the translator has to use two different words for what in the original text is one and the same word. The two meanings, the material and the immaterial, were present side by side, or mingled, in the *one* Greek word.

Now I want to suggest that if we set side by side the two linguistic phenomena which we have been looking at, we see on the one side the thing I spoke of first, the relatively recent tendency to refer to the qualities in the outside world (call it the world of nature, if you like) in terms of their effect upon ourselves. Then you see on the other side a much older habit (I call it a habit, because this time it is too widespread to refer to it as a mere "tendency"), that much older universal habit of referring to ourselves and our thoughts and affections in terms of the world of nature, the outside world. So we see, reflected in language, a curiously equivocal relation between this outside world and the inner man, the self or ego of the human being which experiences it. But we see something more than that. If you survey that equivocal relation, as I've called it, historically, you can't fail to be struck by the fact that there has occurred in the course of ages a change of emphasis. One could really say a change in the center of gravity, a change in direction in the way which this equivocal relation operates. Looking back into the past, we observe an external, an outer language, a material language referring to the outer world of nature, which becomes more and more used in such a way that it becomes an inner language or an immaterial language, as Bentham called it. And this is clearly a very important process, for it is only to the extent that we have a language in which to express a thing that we can really be said to be properly conscious of the thing at all. That may sound a controversial proposition, but I think it's an experience which we all have as children, when our learning to speak on the one hand, and on the other our whole awareness of our environment as a coherent and articulated world, increase side by side as correlatives to one another.

What then was the thing of which this gradual historical development of an inner or immaterial language out of an outer or material language enabled mankind as a whole to become aware? The answer is clear, I think. It was none other than the existence, hitherto unsuspected, of an inner world in contradistinction to the outer one. In other words it was the existence of a man's self as a conscious individual being. Clearly, it was with the help of language—it was through the instrumentality of language—that individual men first began discovering themselves.

But now, what do we imply when we say that something has been "discovered"? If it was discovered at a certain point or during a certain period of time, as it must have been, we imply that there was a previous period during which it was not yet discovered. But please note carefully that, although this must always be the case, it may have been the case for either of two reasons. The thing may have been undiscovered because, although it was already in existence, although it was always there, no one had so far happened to notice it. That's the one reason. Should I be in order, I wonder, here in placing the discovery of America as an example of that category? I don't know. But anyhow, there are plenty of other examples. Take the planet Neptune, for example. That's the first kind of discovery: not discovered because it didn't happen to be noticed although it was already there. But the thing might also have been undiscovered, for a different reason. The reason might be simply that it wasn't yet there. If you discover a new, wild flower in your garden, next spring, let's say it's an annual, the reason you didn't discover it last spring may be that the bird or the wind which carries the seed didn't happen to have passed that way, whereas this year it did. That is the second kind of discovery. We cannot always be certain which of the two causes any particular discovery belongs to. It is conceivable, for instance, that even the planet Neptune *might* not have been in existence until about the time it was discovered, though I expect we are right in classifying that as a discovery of the first kind.

But there is one case where we *can* be absolutely certain that the discovery was *not* of the first kind, and therefore was of the second kind (the discovery of something which did not exist until it was discovered); and that is the discovery by man of his own existence as a self-conscious being. The reason is plain enough. It simply does not make sense to say that at one time self-consciousness was an existing fact which had not yet been discovered. You can be unaware of many things, but you cannot be unaware of being aware. In this case, therefore, the discovery and the birth of the thing discovered are one and the same event.

We see, then, looking back into the past, a condition of affairs in which it was not yet possible to speak of an inner world or an individual self in contradistinction to an outer world. And when this did begin to become possible, the inner world at first could only be suggested by the way in which one employed the language of the outer world. We see this particular way of using words, the (if you like) "symbolical" way, or the way of imagery, gradually growing in strength and variety until there comes into being a whole rich, immaterial language, a rich treasury of words, which had at one time, indeed, an external reference, but from which in common usage, all external reference has long since passed away. That is what we see when we look back into the past. And then we see looking at the present a state of affairs in which the tables have been turned. The tables have been turned in the linguistic relation between man and nature, or between the individual self and its environment. Because, as I pointed out at the beginning, if a man now wants to say anything about his natural environment, anything rich or qualitative, as distinct from the purely quantitative measurements of natural science, he has to do it by employing a language whose literal reference is to something that is going on within himself, but employing it in such a way that he somehow suggests that those qualities exist not in himself, but in the world outside himself.

I have, it is true, given only a single indication of this last, namely, a particular small group of words. There are, in fact, plenty of other indications of what I am saying, but it would take too long to go into them. I'm not, and I should like to make this very clear, attempting to argue a case. I can go no further than stating it.

Now, a change of direction is, by its very nature, a change which must have taken place at a definite point in time. The moment of change may be easily observable, may be easy to determine or locate, or it may not. In the case of a billiard ball hitting the cushion and rebounding, it is easy enough. In the case of a more complex phenomenon, it may be very much harder. The waves, for instance, keep on coming in even after the tide has turned. And an extra large wave may make us doubt whether it has turned yet after all. In the case of an infinitely more complex phenomenon, such as the evolution of human consciousness, it is even less likely that the actual moment of change will be easily observable. But that there *was* such a moment, even though we were unable to locate it exactly, is a conclusion to which reason itself compels us; for otherwise, there could not have been a change of direction at all. Moreover, if the moment of change or reversal cannot be exactly pinpointed, that does not mean that it cannot be placed at all. I don't know the exact moment at which the incoming tide changed to an outflowing one, but I do know that it is an outflowing one now, and that five minutes ago, let's say, it was still coming in.

And now, if I may leave my analogy of the turning of the tide, and return to this change I have been speaking of, this reversal in the direction of man's relation to his environment, this change from a period, in which, with the help of language, man is drawing his self-consciousness, as it were, out of the world around him, to a period in which he is, again, with the help of language, in a position to give back to nature something of the treasure he once took from her, then a student of the history of word meanings can certainly be as definite as this: he can say with confidence that the great change of direction took place between, well, let's say between the death of Alexander the Great and the birth of St. Augustine. Indeed, there are indications which would tempt him to be much more precise.

Again, I'll only give one such indication. If one contrasts the meaning of the Greek word for *word* or *reason* or *discourse* (for it could mean all three: I'm referring to the word *"logos"*), if one contrasts the meaning of that word, as it stood in the time of Plato and Aristotle, with its later meaning; or to put it another way, if one contrasts the meaning of the old word *"logos,"* with the meanings of the words which we have to use to translate it; and if one then moves the microscope a little nearer, so to speak, so as to determine, if possible, the moment, or at least the single century, of transition from the old to the new, then one is struck immediately by the way in which this word *"logos"* was being used, in Alexandria, for instance, used by Greeks and used also by Jews, in the first century B.C. One may even be a little more pedantically precise, and remark that that particular word was in special use in the Stoic philosophy, and that it was in expounding the Stoic philosophy that the concepts *objective* and *subjective* first make their appearance in a clearly recognizable form. In other words, it was then that the fundamental duality with which we are now so familiar was first clearly formulated, was first sharply focused, a duality no longer merely between *mind* on one side and *senses* on the other (which had long been familiar to the Greeks), but a duality between a *self* on the one side and its *environment* on another.

And so, if it were possible (and of course it is not) that a man should have pursued the kind of studies I have been speaking of, without ever having read the Gospels, or the Epistles of St. Paul, without ever having heard of Christianity, he would nevertheless be impelled by his reason to the conclusion that a crucial moment in the evolution of humanity must have occurred certainly during the seven or eight centuries on either side of the reign of Augustus and probably somewhere near the middle of that period. This, he would feel, from the whole course of his studies, was the moment at which the flow of the spiritual tide into the individual self was exhausted and the possibility of an outward flow began. This was the moment at which there was consummated that agelong process of contraction of the immaterial qualities of the cosmos into a human center, into an inner world, which had made possible the development of an immaterial language. This, therefore, was the moment in which his true selfhood, his spiritual selfhood, entered into the body of man. Casting about for a word to denote that moment, what one would he be likely to choose? I think he would be almost obliged to choose the word "incarnation," the entering into the body, the entering into the flesh.

And now let us further suppose that our imaginary student of the history of language, having had up to now that conspicuous gap in his general historical knowledge, was suddenly confronted for the first time with the Christian record; that he now learned for the first time, that at about the middle of the period which his investigation had marked off, a man was born who claimed to be the son of God, and to have come down from Heaven, that he spoke to his followers of the "the Father in me and I in you," that he told all those who stood around him that "the kingdom of God is within you," and startled them, and strove to reverse the direction of their thought—for the word "*metanoia*," which is translated "repentance," also means a reversal of the direction of the mind—he startled them and strove to reverse the direction of their thought by assuring them that "it is not that which cometh into a man which defileth him, but that which goeth out of him."

Lastly, let me further suppose that, excited by what he had just heard, our student made further inquiries and learned that this man, so far from being a charlatan or lunatic, had long been acknowledged, even by those who regarded his claim to have come down from Heaven as a delusion, as the nearest anyone had ever come to being a perfect man. What conclusion do you think our student would be likely to draw?

Well, as I say, the supposition is an impossible one, but it *is* possible—I know because it happened in my own case—for a man to have been brought up in the belief, and to have taken it for granted, that the account given in the Gospels of the birth and the resurrection of Christ is a noble fairy story with no more claim to historical accuracy than any other myth; and it is possible for such a man, after studying in depth the history of the growth of language, to look again at the New Testament and the literature and tradition that has grown up around it, and to accept (if you like, to be *obliged* to accept) the record as a historical fact, not because of the authority of the Church nor by any process of ratiocination such as C. S. Lewis has recorded in his own case, but rather because it fitted so inevitably with the other facts as he had already found them. Rather because he felt, in the utmost humility, that if he had never heard of it through the Scriptures, he would have been obliged to try his best to invent something like it as a hypothesis to save the appearances.

Contributors

Christopher Bamford is the author of *The Voice of the Eagle: The Heart of Celtic Christianity* and *An Endless Trace: The Passionate Pursuit of Wisdom in the West*. He has also translated and edited many other books and is editor-in-chief of SteinerBooks and its imprints.

Owen Barfield (1898–1997) is the author of numerous books, including *Poetic Diction: A Study in Meaning; Romanticism Comes of Age; Unancestral Voice; History in English Words;* and *The Rediscovery of Meaning. Saving the Appearances: A Study in Idolatry* was featured on Philip Zaleski's list of "The 100 Best Spiritual Books of the 20th Century."

Kate Farrell is a poet whose books include *Sleeping on the Wing: An Anthology of Modern Poetry with Essays on Reading and Writing* (written with Kenneth Koch) and *Art & Wonder, An Illustrated Anthology of Visionary Poetry*.

Gertrude Reif Hughes, for many years a Professor of English and Women's Studies at Wesleyan University, is the author of *Emerson's Demanding Optimism*.

Georg Kühlewind (1924–2006), a Hungarian philosopher, was a prolific author who lectured widely. Volumes that have been translated into English include *Becoming Aware of the Logos, From Normal to Healthy,* and *Stages of Consciousness: Meditations on the Boundaries of the Soul*.

Michael Lipson, a clinical psychologist, is the author of *Stairway of Surprise: Six Steps to a Creative Life*. He translated Rudolf Steiner's *Intuitive Thinking as a Spiritual Path* as well as numerous books by Georg Kühlewind.

Jacques Lusseyran (1925-1971) was a French philosopher famous for his heroism in the French Resistance Movement and for his insights into blindness. He is the author of *And There Was Light, Against the Pollution of the I,* and *Conversations Amoureuse*.

Nathan Lyons edited and introduced *Jones Very: Selected Poems*.

Nick Lyons is co-editor of *Educating as an Art: Essays on Waldorf Education*.

Robert McDermott is editor of *The Essential Steiner* and is president emeritus and professor of philosophy and religion at the California Institute of Integral Studies.

George O'Neil and his wife Gisela are coauthors of *The Human Life.*

Andrei Tarkovsky (1932-1986), whose films are known for their metaphysical themes and extraordinary beauty, is widely regarded as one of most important filmmakers in the history of cinema. His films include *Ivan's Childhood, Andrei Rublev, Solaris, The Stalker, Nostalghia,* and *The Sacrifice.*

Andrew Welburn is a fellow of New College, Oxford. His many books include *The Beginnings of Christianity: Essene Mystery, Gnostic Revelation and the Christian Vision* and *Rudolf Steiner's Philosophy and the Crisis of Contemporary Thought.*

John Wulsin edited *The Riddle of America: Essays Exploring America's "Native Expression-Spirit."*

Arthur Zajonc, professor of physics at Amherst College, is the author of *Catching the Light: The Entwined History of Light and Mind.* He edited *The New Physics and Cosmology: Dialogues with the Dalai Lama,* co-edited *Goethe's Way of Science,* and coauthored *The Quantum Challenge.*

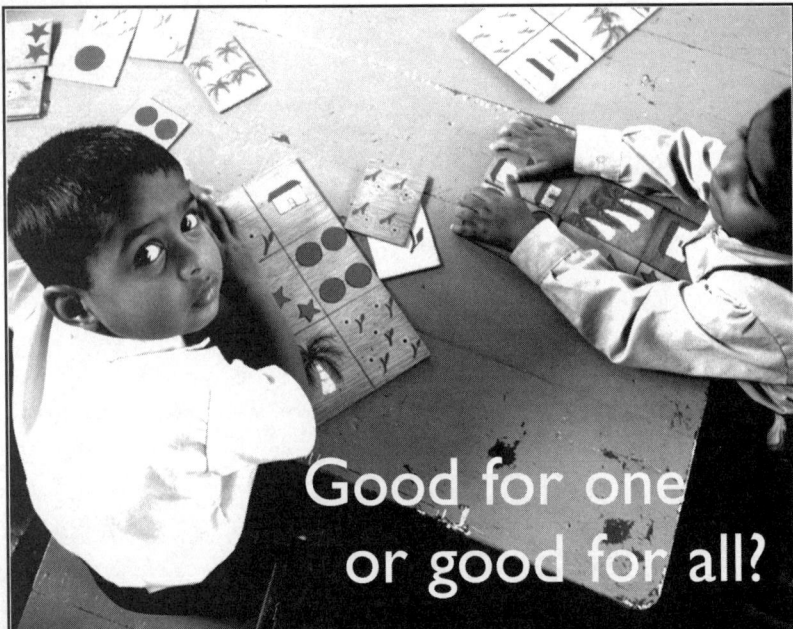

Good for one
or good for all?

Do your investments promote fairness? Or do they perpetuate the status quo?

Fair trade. Education. Biodynamic farming. Organizations that hold the most hope for building a more equitable world have the least access to funds for survival and growth. You can help move them improve the standard of living for those in need by investing with RSF.

Help us provide urgently needed funding for solutions to our planet's most pressing problems. And see the immediate impact of your investment. Coffee farmers earn a living wage and send their children to school. Biodynamic farmers get their food to market.

RSF
Innovations in Social Finance

**Earn a financial return and
help heal the world.**
1-888-RSF-3737
RSFSocialFinance.org

Inspired by the work of Rudolf Steiner

Photo: © Fair Trade Media Foundation courtesy TransFair USA. This is not an offer to sell or the solicitation of an offer to buy. Investments are offered solely through the Prospectus for the RSF Social Investment Fund. No investment may occur from a state in which an offer, solicitation, or sale is not authorized.

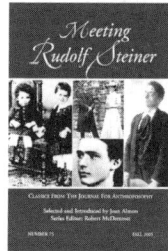

"CLASSIC" SELECTIONS FROM
THE *JOURNAL FOR ANTHROPOSOPHY*

Four very special issues composed of outstanding "classic" selections from the *Journal for Anthroposophy* are scheduled to appear over the next few years. For each volume, a special editor will select and introduce a group of articles that have to do with a specific theme. The selections will be taken from issues dating from as far back as the 1960's.

Robert McDermott is the General Editor of the "Classics" series. The editors of the first two volumes are Joan Almon and Kate Farrell. Existing or new subscribers will receive the "Classic" editions as a part of their subscription. For subscribers in the U.S., two-issue subscriptions are $22.00; mailed to Canada $25.00; mailed overseas $27.00.

These special editions will likely become sought-after because of their unique content and points of view. They will be made widely available. Bookstores can order them on a quantity basis. SteinerBooks will offer them through their catalog and on-line.

The First Volume in the Series – Meeting Rudolf Steiner

Firsthand accounts of living and working with Rudolf Steiner comprise this enticing collection. Steiner's personal qualities are brought to life through descriptions of a wide range of experiences – from intimate memories of Steiner's dinner table humor to vivid reports of the burning of the first Goetheanum. Authors include Albert Schweitzer, Bruno Walter, Arvia MacKay Ege, Andrei Belyi, Lisa Monges.

The volume is edited by Joan Almon, Co-General Secretary of the Anthroposophical Society in America and a former *Journal* editor.

The Second Volume in the Series – Anthroposophy & Imagination

In what way is imagination true? And what can it do for us? This collection reflects the view that true imagination, unlike mere fantasy, is a more-than-rational way of knowing; a natural bridge between matter and spirit; and a transformative state and stage of consciousness, open to us all.

The volume brings together a wide variety of voices: physicist Arthur Zajonc, the great Russian filmmaker Andrei Tarkovsky, philosophers Owen Barfield and Georg Kühlewind, and such authors as Christopher Bamford, Jacques Lusseyran, Gertrude Reif Hughes, Michael Lipson and Andrew Welburn.

Kate Farrell, who edited the issue, is a poet whose books include *Art & Wonder: An Illustrated Anthology of Visionary Poetry* and *Time's River: The Voyage of Life in Art and Poetry.*

Robert McDermott, Series Editor

Robert McDermott, PhD, was president and is currently professor of philosophy and religion at the California Institute of Integral Studies. He was formerly professor and chair of the department of philosophy at Baruch College, CUNY.

Moving?

Please notify us six weeks before you move to ensure that you receive your next *Journal*.

Name _____

Old Address:

Address _____
City/State/Postal Code _____

New Address:

Address _____
City/State/Postal Code _____

Send to: *Journal For Anthroposophy*
             1923 Geddes Ave., Ann Arbor, MI 48104

Journal for ANTHROPOSOPHY

Yes, I would like to subscribe / resubscribe.

I enclose payment of __ $22 USA, __ $25 Canada, __ $27 overseas for a one year (2 issue) subscription.

Name _____

Address _____

City/State/Postal Code _____

Send to: *Journal For Anthroposophy*
             1923 Geddes Ave., Ann Arbor, MI 48104